The Pacific Rim Region

The Pacific Rim Region

A World Marketplace Approach Through Trade and Investment

Chuck Dangler

MADISON BOOKS

Published by Madison Books
4720 Boston Way
Lanham, Maryland 20706

Distributed by National Book Network

The paper used in this publication meets the minimum requirements of American National Standard for Information Sciences—Permanence of Paper for Printed Library Materials, ANSI Z39.48–1984. ∞™
Manufactured in the United States of America.

ISBN 0–8191–8629–5

CONTENTS

LIST OF TABLES

PREFACE

As our procession ventures onward into the twenty-first century, the Pacific Rim Region maintains a firm and expanding influence upon the global marketplace. Accounting for 28.5 percent of world trade and 51 percent of the world's population by 1988, an inclusive Pacific Rim Region geographical consideration continues to elude the private and public sectors in the early 1990s due to political and/or military overtones. Unlike other Pacific Rim Region oriented published evaluations, *The Pacific Rim Region: A World Marketplace Approach Through Trade and Investment* defines, quantifies, and operationalizes the entire Pacific Rim Region for use in the world marketplace.

Through a mixture of geographical and economic considerations, geoeconomics is introduced from the standpoint of evaluating a regional economic market, and serves as the analytical framework for which the Pacific Rim Region is defined, quantified, and operationalized within the global marketplace. This analytical concept transcends political and military overtones, and focuses on a particular area with reference to a geographical feature common to the economic entities being evaluated.

For our purposes, the Pacific Rim Region is the geographic feature common to the forty-six members considered here. The Pacific Rim Region includes independent nation-states and other resourceful economic entities that abut, and are adjacent to, the Pacific Ocean. The multicultural, economically viable Pacific Rim Region ranges from the Pacific Ocean shores of South, Central, and North America, to East Asia, Australia, and the majority of the Pacific Island States. Instead of exclusively focusing on political preferences that influence economic activity in the Pacific Rim Region, economic indicators and geographical considerations are utilized as basic factors in economic development. Therefore, geographical-economics, or geoeconomics, is employed when discussing the Pacific Rim Region; where geographic boundaries and geographic implications serve as the framework for an economic market, or group of economic markets. To some degree, this idea falls within the integrated market category in today's world; for example, the European Communities (EC), the Central American Common Market (CACM), the Association of Southeast Asian Nations (ASEAN), the European Free Trade Association (EFTA), and the

Colombo Plan. Common economic goals, a geographical proximity to one another, and/or similar international market perspectives tend to attract member nations together to form an integrated, or common market. As for geographic implications within the geoeconomic perspective, geographical features influence economic activities and environmental conditions. These influences range from choice of fuels, types of building construction, to modes of transportation, and income producing activities. In other words, in geoeconomics, geographical influences play a major role where the historical, political development is an element rather than the main focus of economic development.

Within a global context, a clear, concise Pacific Rim Region conceptual framework is timely. As the parameters of the General Agreement on Tariffs and Trade (GATT) are challenged with rising trade protectionism and emerging regional economic groupings, a well-defined Pacific Rim Region and a pragmatic Pacific Rim Region economic and trade organization could provide insight into effective regional economic groupings. Instead of acting as a breeding ground for trade protectionism, a regional economic grouping can enhance economic development and economic activity, while ultimately enabling member economies to offer a larger selection of goods, services, and purchasing power within the world marketplace.

With a balanced, well-measured approach to protect domestic markets within a regional economic grouping, trade protectionism could act as a positive influence rather than an overbearing hinderance to international trade; providing such trade restrictions are maintained at levels compatible to meet the supply requirements of a member's economy without substantially hindering domestic industries. Unfortunately, trade protectionism is inexorably imbued within international commerce. To what degree trade protectionism is utilized determines the international effectiveness of our domestic economies, and ultimately, the international economy. Analogously, when water behind a hydroelectric dam is released in a well-managed fashion, the kinetic energy can be utilized effectively. Otherwise, kinetic energy is wasted because of insufficient water flows through the dam, or an over-abundance of water passing through the dam could create water and energy shortages for the future. Similar to managing a dam, trade protectionism can be managed effectively. When managed effectively, trade protectionism can be utilized to our advantage through the benefits of a balanced, coordinated approach sensitive to international commerce activity. Otherwise, mismanaged trade protectionism can be disastrous as prior to the Second World War when trade protectionism was so fierce most national economies were isolated from the international marketplace, which fueled persistent, depressed levels of domestic production, employment, and purchasing power. Even with the 1948 inception of GATT, regional economic groupings continue to emerge. Within this atmosphere, a clearly defined, quantified, and operational approach to the entire Pacific Rim Region would prove profitable and advantageous to international commerce.

The operational aspect of this book defines the Pacific Rim Region in relation to the Equator and the International Date Line, and encompasses the four directional quarters of the Pacific Ocean. The Pacific Rim Region Trade and Economic Organization (PRRTEO), pronounced "per-tea-o", is also introduced. With adequate support and funding from business, government, and the Region's citizens, the benefits generated through PRRTEO would efficaciously enrich the Pacific Rim Region. Dedicated to the profitable benefits of peace, trade, direct investment, and understanding, PRRTEO auspiciously espouses a forum for the open exchange of ideas, and to provide for the exchange of trade and economic information in order to enhance trade and investment activities within the Region. Even if favorable tariff rates and coordinated trade policies prove unmanageable through PRRTEO, that is fine; because paramount to a diversified, forty-six member multilateral organization is to pursue and *maintain* the open exchange of information and ideas. As long as avenues of communication remain open, an expanding awareness of the members will evolve, which will eventually foster enhanced trade and investment activities throughout the Region. For through understanding, the benefits are immense and, at times, difficult to quantify.

In an effort to avoid "over-analysis," this book was designed to present a straight-forward evaluation of the Pacific Rim Region filled with relevant international trade and international investment figures. This approach will enable you to make informed conclusions about the emerging Pacific Rim Region. For those inclined to use an outline, you'll find the Contents useful. Once the Region is defined, examined from an advantage/disadvantage perspective, and presented along with previous inadequate definitions laden with political overtones, the

Pacific Rim Region's diversified international commercial activity is then evaluated. Bilateral trade figures to and from the world, financial flows, and investment trends during the 1978-88 period are considered through a statistical compilation of the forty-six Pacific Rim Region economies. Major trade policies, and trade arrangements, for the predominant economy in each of the four Quarters of the Region — Japan, Australia, Chile, and the United States — are discussed.

To coordinate and utilize the above information and Pacific Rim Region concept in a practical fashion, an operational approach for a regional economic and trade organization is introduced. With respect to economic considerations, instead of political and/or military alliances, the Pacific Rim Region Trade and Economic Organization provides an organizational format facilitating peace, trade, direct investment, and understanding. Headquartered in the center of the Region, with various satellite offices among the Region's four Quarters, PRRTEO activities would include:

- to nourish a Pacific Rim Region community atmosphere through a forum for the open exchange of ideas;

- to enhance economic activity and economic growth among member economies through the timely exchange of economic, trade, commercial, and investment activity trends about member economies, and the world marketplace;

- to disseminate the above economic, trade, commercial, and investment activity information among the private and public sectors in the Region within a timely fashion, and;

- to consider forming a loose economic association by either coordinating trade and economic policies, instituting preferential tariff treatments, or through trade liberalization programs.

Within this PRRTEO and Pacific Rim Region context, *The Pacific Rim Region: A World Marketplace Approach Through Trade and Investment* concludes with the Region's economic prospects leading into the global market of the twenty-first century.

Reflecting the emergence of the regional trade agreement trend, new approaches and new ideas are offered in this book toward defining and operationalizing a regional economic grouping within the world marketplace. By chance this work engenders a genuine Pacific Rim Region community atmosphere — concerned with the profitable benefits of peace, trade, direct investment, and understanding — then this book served its purpose.

Chuck Dangler

Spring 1992
Kitsap County, Washington

This book is dedicated to the
open exchange of ideas, the multifaceted
perspectives an open exchange inherently offers, and
to the auspicious nature of genuine understanding . . .

CHAPTER ONE

Introduction

Evolving as a new international community concept, the Pacific Rim Region lacks a common geographical definition, and consequently, an economic conceptual framework among the private and public sectors. Countering this ambiguity, this book focuses on a clear, concise, conceptual framework which defines, quantifies, and places the Pacific Rim Region in a practical context for operational use within the world marketplace.

There are numerous reasons for considering the Pacific Rim Region. The reasons are multifaceted and prove advantageous from a variety of perspectives. These perspectives are fourfold: 1) to help define the emerging Pacific Rim Region in the international business community, 2) to capitalize on the multilateral, post-World War II trading arrangement trend, 3) to acknowledge that trans-Pacific commerce continues to exceed trans-Atlantic commerce since 1982, and 4) within this atmosphere is an opportunity to enhance economic activity and economic growth through a proposed Pacific Rim Region Trade and Economic Organization. When the Pacific Rim Region term emerged as a "buzz-word" in the business community in the late 1970s, an assortment of definitions ensued in the private and public sectors. Ask any colleague to define the region, and you will find with each person a different definition exists. To counter this ambiguity, a geographically accurate definition of the Pacific Rim Region is offered here. Also, with reference to international trade figures, and major investment trends among the four most economically active members (in terms of output and international trade activity), the Pacific Rim Region is clearly quantified in the 1978-1988 period.

Since World War II, multilateral and bilateral regional trade agreements have evolved. By 1990, an assortment of regional trade agreements were in force which, in some instances, encompassed political and security interests as well. Among these successful agreements include: the Colombo Plan, the European Communities, the European Free Trade Association, and the Association of South East Asian Nations. Originally established by seven Commonwealth nations in 1950, the Colombo Plan is comprised of twenty-six nations.

Currently, the Colombo Plan pursues three objectives: promotes and supports the economic and social interest in Asia and the Pacific; reviews the economic and social development in the region and assists with accelerating development through cooperative effort; and facilitates development to and within the region. Membership ranges from Afghanistan, Canada, and Fiji, to India, Japan, Malaysia, Papua New Guinea, and the United States.[1] The European Communities embody three treaties which, in essence, form a loose confederation and a customs union. Until 1967, the three Communities created by the European Coal and Steel Community (ECSC), the European Atomic Energy Community (EAEC or EURATOM), and the European Economic Community (EEC) operated separately through shared nondecision-making bodies. By 1991, the EC included twelve members and now is attempting to establish a common currency acceptable to all members. The EC goals are: to ensure peace through combining mutual interests; gradual economic integration; and movement toward closer political unity. The European Communities consist of Belgium, France, the Federal Republic of Germany, Italy, Luxembourg, the Netherlands, the United Kingdom, Ireland, Denmark, Greece, Spain, and Portugal.

Nine years following the commencement of the ECSC agreement, the European Free Trade Association (EFTA) was enacted in 1960. Today, the six member EFTA includes Austria, Finland, Iceland, Norway, Sweden, and Switzerland. All three of EFTA's objectives were accomplished by abolishing most tariffs within the EFTA, assisting with creating a single market among the countries of Western Europe, and contributing to the expansion of world trade. In 1959, trade among current EFTA members amounted to $706 million with total exports at $6.6 billion. In 1988, inter-EFTA trade and EFTA exports accounted for $25 billion and $117 billion, respectively.

By August 1967, the Association of South East Asian Nations (ASEAN) formed to: ensure the stability of the South East Asian region; to accelerate economic growth, social progress, and cultural development; to promote active collaboration and mutual assistance in matters of common interest; and to maintain close cooperation with existing international and regional organizations with similar aims. In 1984, Brunei joined ASEAN's original five nation membership: Indonesia, Malaysia, the Philippines, Singapore, and Thailand.[2]

Other reasons for considering the Pacific Rim Region rests with the absolute international trade activity traversing the Pacific Ocean, and the opportunity to enhance economic activity and economic growth among Pacific Rim Region members through a Pacific Rim Region Trade and Economic Organization. In 1982, trans-Pacific trade of $112 billion exceeded trans-Atlantic trade by $12 billion. By 1989, trans-Pacific trade amounted to about $300 billion where trans-Atlantic trade totaled $115 billion. The economic trend is clear. Export-oriented growth of the newly industrializing economies (NIEs) and Japan continues to contribute to the shift from the once predominant trans-Atlantic trade to trans-Pacific trade. Regional trade agreements and expanding regional trade activity has influenced international trade activity in the Pacific Rim Region as well. For example, Australia is considered a prime raw material supplier for Japan and the NIEs, and the Caribbean Basin area benefits from preferential tariff treatment from the United States through the Caribbean Basin Initiative (CBI). Coupled with the current Enterprise of the Americas Initiative, proposed by the United States, the entire Western Hemisphere may enjoy the benefits of a free trade area in the decades ahead.

Yet, amidst these prodigious economic developments in the Pacific Rim Region community, few private and public sector organizations openly acknowledge the entire Pacific Rim Region membership. Those organizations that do acknowledge the Pacific Rim Region concept are select with their membership and omit economies that are present in the Pacific Rim Region. The Asia Pacific Economic Cooperation Forum (APEC) and the Pacific Economic Cooperation Conference (PECC) tout the Pacific term in their name, but in practice favor only the few larger economies in the Pacific Region. In fact, PECC recently offered associate memberships to Mexico and Chile instead of full memberships. Both nations declined. Only the Pacific Basin Economic Council (PBEC), a private sector business organization, offered full membership to Chile, Peru, and Mexico in 1988. However, the PBEC focuses their activities in East Asia, primarily among ASEAN members. In an effort to enhance economic activity in the Pacific Rim Region community (without discriminatory membership practices with respect to any economy located in the Pacific Rim Region), and to utilize the flourishing multilateral trade agreement atmosphere, a Pacific Rim Region Trade and Economic Organization is introduced in this book.

In order to avoid "over-analysis," this Pacific Rim Region evaluation simply provides a clear definition and an operational framework for the Pacific Rim Region that would enhance economic activity and economic growth. In essence, the analytical approach is two pronged in nature. Through basic geographical and economic considerations (geoeconomics), the Pacific Rim Region is inclusively defined. As for operationalizing the Pacific Rim Region, the customs union theory is applied in order to substantiate a Pacific Rim Region Trade and Economic Organization aimed at enhancing economic performance and understanding throughout the Region.

The geoeconomic approach is a novel analytical perspective from the standpoint of evaluating a regional economic market, and is introduced here when defining the Pacific Rim Region. This analytical concept transcends political and military overtones, and focuses on a particular area with reference to a geographic feature common to the economic entities being evaluated. For our purposes, the Pacific Rim Region is the common geographic feature common to the forty-six members considered here. Instead of exclusively focusing on political preferences which influence economic activity in the Pacific Rim Region, economic indicators and geographical considerations are utilized as basic factors in economic development. Therefore, geographical-economics, or geoeconomics, is employed when discussing the Pacific Rim Region; where geographic boundaries and geographic implications serve as the framework for an economic market, or group of economic markets. To some degree, this idea falls within the integrated market category in today's world; for example, the European Communities, the Central American Common Market, the Association of Southeast Asian Nations, the European Free Trade Association, and the Colombo Plan. Common economic goals, a geographic proximity to one another, and/or similar international market perspectives tend to attract member nations together to form an integrated, or common market. As for geographic implications within the geoeconomic perspective, geographical features influence economic activities and environmental conditions. These influences range from choice of fuels, types of building construction, to modes of transportation, and income producing activities. In other words, in geoeconomics, geographical influences play a major role where the historical, political development is an element rather than the main focus of economic development.

By applying this basic geoeconomic perspective — transcending political and military overtones — the Pacific Rim Region is defined with reference to independent nations, and other viable economic entities which abut, or are adjacent to, the Pacific Ocean. The Pacific Rim Region, also referred to as the Region, is comprised of forty-two independent nation-states along with Hong Kong, New Caledonia, French Polynesia, and the Republic of Palau, totaling forty-six Region members. In relation to the International Date Line and the Equator, the Pacific Rim Region encompasses the four directional quarters: the Northwest Quarter, the Southwest Quarter, the Southeast Quarter, and the Northeast Quarter.

For each Quarter, a predominant economy is identified in order to better evaluate each Quarter, and the Pacific Rim Region as a whole. Although these four economies may prove other than overriding economic influences in their respective Quarters, they certainly provide substantial economic influences among neighboring economies. Such economic influences include international trade and direct investment activity. Due to the ranking, absolute value of their economic output, and international trade figures, respective of each others Quarter members; Japan, Australia, Chile, and the United States are identified as the four predominant economies in the Pacific Rim Region. By identifying these predominant economies in the Region, these four economies serve as "handles," or "quantifiable pillars," for which to decisively grasp the Pacific Rim Region's predominant economic activity.

From an operational standpoint, the customs union principle substantiates the economic benefits generated through regional trade agreements. In this instance, we are referring to the Pacific Rim Region Trade and Economic Organization introduced here to enhance economic performance and understanding in the Region. The theory of the customs union embodies a unique position in the field of international trade theory and entails two interpretive perspectives: 1) as a special discipline within international trade, and 2) as a specific case of the analysis of economic integration. Broadly speaking, a customs union includes collaborative efforts by two or more countries in order to mutually increase the economic performance among member economies through reducing tariffs, and coordinating trade and economic policies. Specific measures initiated through a customs union are simply inherent to the participants involved and the goals they wish to ascertain. As a result, a spacious spectrum exists when defining a customs union. One side of the spectrum represents a mutual reduction of protectionism on one or more products among a specific number of countries. The other side of the spectrum depicts complete trade liberalization and abolition of tariffs, combined with the coordination of internal policies along with the possibility for a newly created common currency.[3] Depending on the information source, various terms to describe the degrees of integration vary considerably. In practical terms, different degrees of integration, or customs union, includes the free trade area, a common market, and an economic union.

For our purposes, integration involves some degree of cooperation and information exchange that may assist in discrimination and mutual trade liberalization to enhance the economic performance among member economies. Although the degrees of integration vary, EFTA and the EC have enjoyed larger terms of trade since the establishment of their respective organizations. Yet, encumbered by the dependency theory dogma, the Latin American Free Trade Area subscribed to import substitution policies vis-à-vis strong protectionism. Created in February 1960, the Latin American Free Trade Area (LAFTA) embraced this philosophy and missed valuable export opportunities in the 1970s and 1980s that were earned by East Asia instead.[4] In an effort to reorganize LAFTA's infidelities, the Latin American Integration Association (LAIA) supplanted LAFTA in 1981, and tariff adjustments among individual countries were based on levels of development. Levels of development include: the more-developed as Argentina, Brazil, Mexico; the medium-developed as Chile, Colombia, Peru, Uruguay, Venezuela; and the less-developed as Bolivia, Ecuador, and Paraguay. With respect to new trade agreements among LAIA members, more developed countries are obligated to grant poorer countries preferential treatment. In the final analysis, the success of a customs union is directly proportional to the degree of integration and the management capabilities of each economy involved.

In view of a Pacific Rim Region Trade and Economic Organization enhanced economic performance opportunities would be viable through a loose economic association fostering economic, trade, commercial, and investment information about each member economy. Allowing common sense to dictate, a more knowledgeable understanding of the Pacific Rim Region and its inhabitants would inevitably evolve among the Region's diversified forty-six members through the frequent exchange of economic information and ideas. In turn, the Pacific Rim Region Trade and Economic Organization would be dedicated to peace, trade, direct investment, and understanding. PRRTEO activities would include:

- to nourish a Pacific Rim Region community atmosphere through a forum for the open exchange of ideas;

- to enhance economic activity and economic growth among member economies through the timely exchange of economic, trade, commercial, and investment activity trends about member economies and the world marketplace;

- to disseminate the above economic, trade, commercial, and investment activity information among the private and public sectors in the Region within a timely fashion, and;

- to consider forming a loose economic association by either coordinating trade and economic policies, instituting preferential tariff treatments, or through trade liberalization programs.

Unifying the Pacific Rim Region concept, geoeconomics, and the Pacific Rim Region Trade and Economic Organization is a common goal, economic prosperity. In today's world, economic prosperity — in terms of national values and cultural beliefs — appears as a common goal among nation-state governments and their citizens. By utilizing this commonality, one can easily discern the fundamental philosophical tenant pervading geoeconomics and the Pacific Rim Region for which it defines. Interpreting economic prosperity differs from culture to culture. At times, some cultures share similar economic prosperity values. For instance, Australia and the United States share similar economic prosperity values; they strongly favor obtaining material wealth and operate within a money-oriented economy. In contrast, approximately 80 percent of Papua New Guineans live outside of the money economy. "Big-men," men who own large gardens and other essential items as boars, represent economic prosperity in Papua New Guinea and wield considerable economic influence. The Chamorros, of the Northern Mariana Islands in the Northwest Pacific, are disinclined to earn retail profits from their own people. Due to their cultural values, the Chamorros accept earning their domestic retail profits from visitors rather than burdening their own people with substantial profit margins. Even though various cultures perceive economic prosperity through their unique cultural preferences, economic prosperity, and what it offers, is the unifying element that serves as the understated primary objective for which to practically pursue the Pacific Rim Region.

Before we explore the organization of this book, we will hopefully satisfy those wishing to evaluate the advantages and disadvantages of this Pacific Rim Region approach. The advantages clearly exceed the disadvantages. The advantages abound when evaluating the Pacific Rim Region concept. An increased market share among members, in terms of international trade and direct investment, translates into expanding economic development and increased income potential: favorable trade mechanisms among members, as lower tariffs and other cost-oriented incentives, stimulates trade; through an ongoing, informal dialogue, an opportunity for member nations to exchange ideas openly — transcending political and military overtones — eventually promotes understanding among members, thus opening more doors for wider trade relations; and utilizing this Pacific Rim Region concept would also prove propitious as a fine counter to the emerging 1992 European Communities market.

Obversely, the disadvantages exhibit inaction and the unwillingness to acknowledge a profitable venture through regional trade agreements when adequately managed. One perceived disadvantage concerns the sheer size of the project at hand. To thoroughly evaluate forty-six member economies, within a regional context, would simply prove absurd unless an international organization was specifically designed to accomplish such a task. In order to justify an area as immense and multifaceted as the Pacific Rim Region, this discussion specifically focuses on a) providing a practical, conceptual framework for the Pacific Rim Region, and b) evaluating international trade activity and major investment trends with respect to the four Pacific Rim Region's predominant economies. Within the context of the world's profitable regional trade arrangements, disadvantages could easily include: missed opportunities among member nations to enhance profits, if regional trade mechanisms are unused, thus impeding economic growth; and the unwillingness among member countries to stimulate and coordinate trade and investment contacts during an era in history when integrated markets are emerging — and prospering — when efficiently managed. Subsequently, the economic benefits clearly outweigh the disadvantages of inaction, and to avoid membership and/or participation in an efficiently managed regional trade arrangement would prove disadvantageous in today's world marketplace.

Economic prosperity, in terms of national values and cultural beliefs, serves as a discreet impetus to entice and maintain interest in the Pacific Rim Region and geoeconomics. Tapping into this common goal embodies the objective of this written account, which clearly defines the Pacific Rim Region concept, along with a regional organization to practically enhance peace, trade, direct investment, and understanding in the Region. Within the geoeconomic perspective, as explained in this introduction, the Region is defined and presented along with previous inadequate Pacific Rim Region definitions laden with political overtones. From this vantage point, the Region's diversified international commercial activity is then evaluated in terms of bilateral trade figures to and from the world, financial flows, and investment trends during the 1978-1988 period through a statistical compilation of the Pacific Rim Region economies. Major trade policies, and trade arrangements, for the predominant economy in each of the four Quarters of the Region — Japan, Australia, Chile, and the United States — are then discussed. In order to coordinate and utilize the above information and Pacific Rim Region concept in a practical fashion, an operational approach for a regional economic and trade organization is introduced for use in the world marketplace. With respect to economic considerations, instead of political and/or military alliances, the Pacific Rim Region Trade and Economic Organization provides an organizational format facilitating peace, trade, direct investment, and understanding. Within this Pacific Rim Region and PRRTEO context, the concluding comments incorporate the Region's economic prospects leading into the global market of the twenty-first century.

For the sake of consistency, all monetary figures are denominated in United States dollars, unless otherwise indicated. In order to provide a diversified, yet reputable statistical perspective, International Monetary Fund, World Bank, United Nations, and national statistics are strongly favored. As for those inclined to utilize an outline, you will find the Contents useful, augmented with the List of Tables and a map. Included in the Appendix is an informative table for the 1978 and 1988 major export and import partners for all Pacific Rim Region members.

CHAPTER TWO

The Pacific Rim Region Clearly Defined

Through a geoeconomic perspective — transcending political and/or military posturing — the Pacific Rim Region is defined with reference to independent nations, and other resourceful economic entities which abut, or are adjacent to, the Pacific Ocean. Before thoroughly elaborating on the methodology and definition of the Pacific Rim Region, for the sake of perspective, consider the Pacific Ocean's presence. With 70.2 percent of water covering the earth, the Pacific Ocean's 69,370,000 square miles, or 179,680,000 square kilometers, contributes 49.7 percent to the total water coverage. In terms of total world surface area, the Pacific Ocean, including its marginal seas, accounts for 35.2 percent of the earth's total 510,072,000 square kilometer surface area. By far, the Pacific Ocean is the largest geographical feature on the planet. As for the Pacific Ocean's marginal seas, they are located in the proximity of East Asia: the Bering Sea, the Sea of Okhotsk, the Sea of Japan, the Yellow Sea, the East China Sea, and the South China Sea. According to the International Hydrographic Organization: the Pacific, Atlantic, and Indian Oceans are the only relatively separate and distinct oceans as compared to the Antarctic and Arctic Oceans.

Traveling northward from southern Chile along the South, Central, and North American coasts, onward along the northeast Asian coast, and southward skirting Southern Asia toward New Zealand, is a horseshoe configuration known as the Pacific Rim. This Pacific Rim is known among geologists and volcanologists as the "Ring of Fire," or the "Pacific Rim of Fire," due to its frequent volcanic and earthquake activity. To date, the Ring of Fire contains 75 percent of the world's 850 active volcanoes, including 20 percent in Indonesia. Other concentrated groupings are located in the Aleutian Islands, Japan, and Central America. Thanks to Dan McKenzie and Robert Parker's conceptual and analytical understanding of plate tectonics, which revolutionized earth movement theories, we now know that most volcanic activity is found within the areas of tectonic plate meeting zones. With reference to the Pacific Rim, in general terms, Pacific Ocean-oriented plates are surrounded by various continental plates. Located south of Guam, the Pacific Rim Region also claims the deepest ocean depth, Challenger Deep, in the Mariana Trench at a depth of 6.86 miles (32,200 feet) or 11,034 kilometers.

Continuing with the definition of the Pacific Rim Region from a geoeconomic standpoint, the Pacific Rim Region is also referred to as the Region. The Region is comprised of forty-two independent nation-states along with Hong Kong, New Caledonia, French Polynesia, and the Republic of Palau, totaling 46 Region members. In relation to the International Date Line and the Equator, the Pacific Rim Region encompasses four directional quarters: the Northwest Quarter, the Southwest Quarter, the Southeast Quarter, and the Northeast Quarter (Please See Map). Nations such as Myanmar (formerly Burma), Laos, and Kampuchea, for example, are included due to their:

- geographic proximity to the Region,
- subsequent economic involvement with newly industrializing economies such as Singapore, Malaysia, Indonesia and Thailand, and
- common location on the Mekong Peninsula which abuts the Pacific Rim Region to the west.

Hong Kong and New Caledonia — although dependencies — were also included in the Region due to their distinctive, international economic stature, the largest free-trade zone and leading nickel producer, respectively. The Republic of Palau, the only remaining member of the Pacific Islands Trust Territory, administered by the United States through a United Nations charter, continues to debate their political relationship with the United States. To date, in the shadow of seven unsuccessful plebiscites, Palau is considering a Free Association with the United States. Amidst Palau's political debate, independence appears imminent and that island state is acknowledged as a resourceful economic entity in the Region. Other Pacific Island locations such as Niue, the Cook Islands, Pitcairn, Easter Island, Norfolk Island, Wallis and Futuna, Tokelau, and the Northern Marianas were avoided due to their political dependency status and paucity of economic activity.

As with any new analytical tool, relevant questions and concerns always arise. There are some instances where certain members of a Quarter may be more suited socially and/or economically to a neighboring Quarter instead of the one they are currently designated in. Because of the immense size of the Pacific Rim Region, all economies in a particular Quarter are designated by their geographic location with reference to the Equator and the International Date Line. In an effort to generate and maintain a genuine Pacific Rim Region spirit, certain member combinations within a particular Quarter are unusual, but plausible within the Pacific Rim Region's Quarter system parameters. For example, Western Samoa and French Polynesia are designated with the Southeast Quarter instead of the Southwest Quarter, and the Federated States of Micronesia and the Marshall Islands are designated with the Northwest Quarter (rather than the Northeast Quarter) even though they both use the United States dollar as their national currency. Although some members appear more socially and/or economically aligned with other members of a neighboring Quarter than within their own Quarter, it would prove inappropriate to over-emphasize this relationship within this analytical context. Inappropriate, in that, Quarter designations are only used to conceptually analyze an immense, economically viable region instead of serving as surmountable boundaries laden with social and/or economic implications.

Within each Pacific Rim Region Quarter, a predominant economy is identified with respect to leading economic output figures and international trade activity. Since output figures and international trade activity usually reflect fundamental economic activity and economic development, to some degree, these economic indicators seem appropriate when classifying a predominant economy for each of the four Quarters. Presented in a counter-clockwise direction, Japan is the predominant economy in the Northwest Quarter, where Australia, Chile, and the United States are the predominant economies in the Southwest, Southeast, and Northeast Quarters, respectively.

Other Definitions and Variations of the Pacific Rim Region Theme

References to a Pacific Rim Region in the literature of the western world ranges from sparse, vaguely defined, to geographically benighted due to political and/or strategic reasons. In fact, a practical, geographically accurate Pacific Rim Region trade and economic conceptual framework has yet to be operationalized in the world marketplace. For the sake of perspective, following is a Pacific Rim Region conceptual cross-section among the academic, business, and government sectors. Although far from definitive, this cross-section will exhibit the elusive nature of the Pacific Rim Region concept.

Responding to the request of the United States Subcommittee of East Asian and Pacific Affairs in the Foreign Relations Committee, the Congressional Research Service initiated an evaluation process for a Pacific area economic association. Modeled after the Organization for Economic Cooperation and Development (OECD), Professors Peter Drysale of the Australian National University and Hugh Patrick of Yale University recommended the creation of an Organization for Pacific Trade and Development (OPTAD) in a July 1979 report. The report addressed the interests of the United States leadership role in the region along with Japan, Australia, and ASEAN members. OPTAD would have functioned as a government organization in order to act as a stimulus for new investments, to facilitate trade, and to encourage a forum for cooperation in the region among market economies. Geographically, OPTAD's fourteen charter members included the United States, Japan, Australia, Canada, New Zealand, ASEAN (Indonesia, Malaysia, Philippines, Singapore, Thailand), South Korea, Taiwan, and Hong Kong. Papua New Guinea and the small Southwest Pacific states were considered as one group. Other membership options were the South Asian nations, Latin American Pacific States plus Brazil, and non-market economies.[5]

Pacific Rim: Investment, Trade, and Development and *Pacific Rim: Area of Change, Area of Opportunity* avoid defining, quantifying, or operationalizing the *entire* Pacific Rim Region for use in the world marketplace. *The Pacific Rim: Investment, Trade, and Development* is a coordinated effort by scholars from Canada, Japan, Thailand, Australia, and Hawaii. Attributing a significant proportion of the Pacific Basin's economic vitality to Japan, this edited edition evaluates trade, investment, development patterns and future economic prospects. This book's other goal explores the role of energy from a supply and demand perspective within the context of "the future development of the Pacific Rim and its interdependence with other global regions." Complete with excellent documentation and a fine assortment of tables, *The Pacific Rim: Investment, Trade, and Development* defines the Pacific Rim as a twenty-four country grouping among "distinct national subgroupings" which include: Oceania, Japan, and the Island States. Aware of the enormity and scope of the Pacific Rim geographically, *Pacific Rim: Area of Change, Area of Opportunity* concedes the Pacific Rim consists of fifteen countries: the United States, Canada, and their thirteen principle trading partners in East Asia and Southeast Asia. East and Southeast Asia are examined within the text, particularly

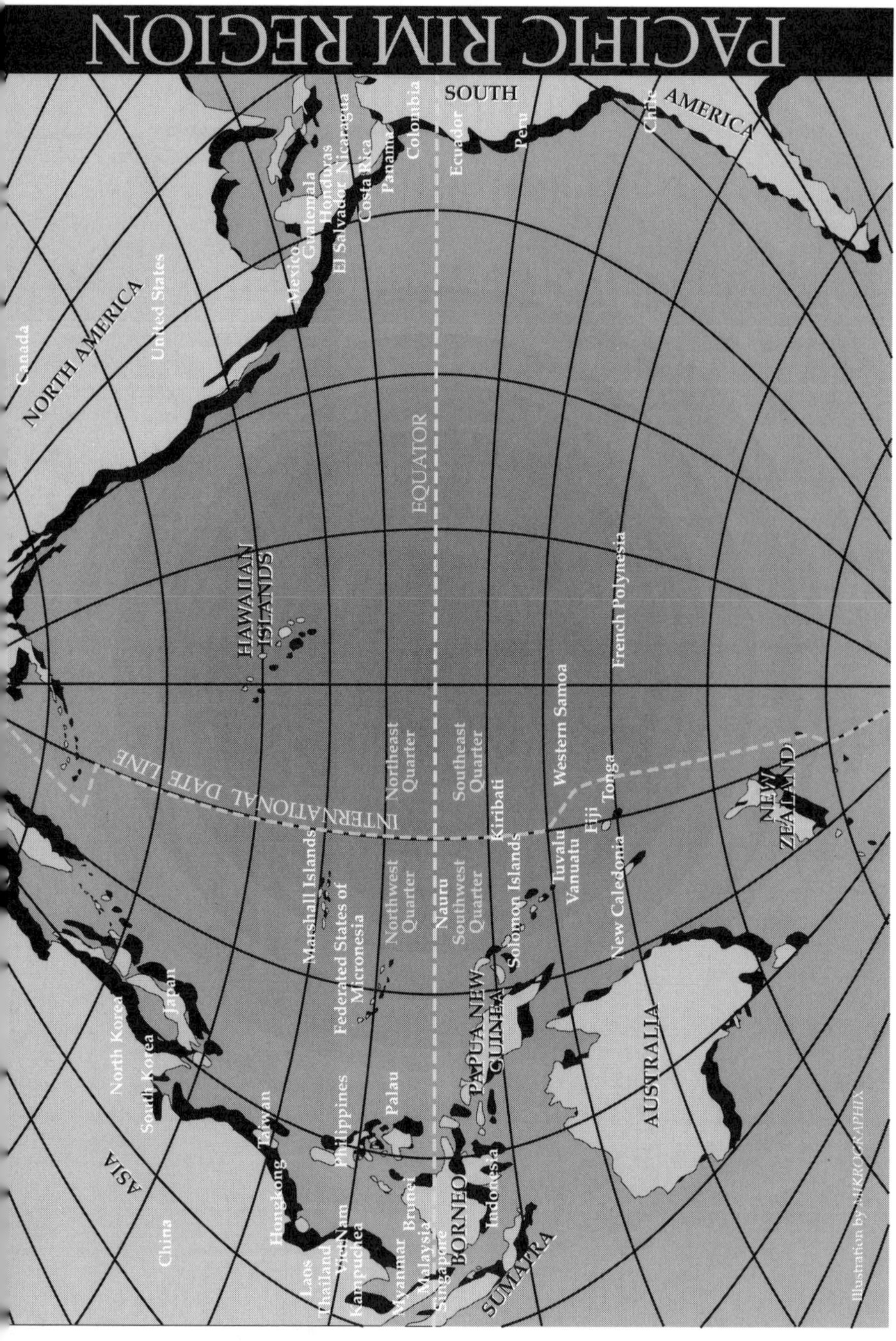
PACIFIC RIM REGION
SOUTH
AMERICA
Chile
Peru
Ecuador
Colombia
Panama
Costa Rica
Nicaragua
Honduras
El Salvador
Guatemala
Mexico
United States
Canada
NORTH AMERICA
EQUATOR
HAWAIIAN ISLANDS
French Polynesia
Western Samoa
Tonga
Fiji
INTERNATIONAL DATE LINE
Northeast Quarter
Southeast Quarter
Kiribati
NEW ZEALAND
Tuvalu
Vanuatu
New Caledonia
Marshall Islands
Federated States of Micronesia
Northwest Quarter
Nauru
Southwest Quarter
Solomon Islands
PAPUA NEW GUINEA
AUSTRALIA
Japan
North Korea
South Korea
Palau
Philippines
Taiwan
ASIA
China
Hongkong
Brunei
Indonesia
BORNEO
Laos
Thailand
Viet Nam
Kampuchea
Myanmar
Malaysia
Singapore
SUMATRA
Illustration by MIKROGRAPHIX

Korea, China, Hong Kong, Taiwan, the Philippines, Vietnam, and Thailand. This book is eloquently presented through a political prism in a journalistic manner, while availing the commercial opportunities specifically for Americans.

Douglas Phillips and Steven Levi offer a refreshing, geographically accurate interpretation of the Pacific Rim in *The Pacific Rim Region*: *Emerging Giant*; arcing northward along the Pacific shores from Chile, to the southwestern Pacific in a horseshoe-shape fashion including numerous Pacific Island markets. This treatment of Pacific Rim member markets coincides with this author's geographic consideration save Laos, Myanmar, and the Republic of Palau. *The Pacific Rim Region: Emerging Giant* deals with the cultural and economic diversities inherent to the Pacific Rim through a juvenile reader's perspective. Filled with interesting historical facts and cultural comparisons, this book — and its Pacific Rim Region definition — is descriptive and well-written for its intended purpose.

In addition to these books, there are two other distinguished works which deal with the Pacific Rim (or a variation of the Pacific Rim Region theme) in terms of political and/or military overtones replete with corresponding geographic considerations. From a geographical context, these works offer an inaccurate and the absence of a definition, respectively, of the Pacific Rim due to overriding political and/or military overtones. *Pacific Basin: Concept and Challenge* presents the United States public policy atmosphere inherent to various Western Pacific Island States, East and South East Asia, including Australia and New Zealand. The primary focus involves Japan, China, and a call for a new Pacific Policy. *The Emerging Pacific Community, A Regional Perspective*, was a multinational conference in Washington, D.C. in October 1983. The "development of trade and high-technology, and the area's security needs" were discussed among leaders and specialists of the community. Roles of the United States, Western Europe, and the Asian nations were explored in the Pacific Basin context. Although an "undaunted optimism" about the general Pacific Basin concept prevailed; membership, a community focus, and degree of integration never materialized.

Other variations of the inclusive Pacific Rim Region concept and terminology (such as Pacific, Pacific Basin, or Asia-Pacific) do exist more in a cognitive, rhetorical fashion than in an ongoing operational, practical venue. While some organizations claim a Pacific-oriented label, in practice they only focus on a few Pacific Rim members.

Following the September 1980 Pacific Community Seminar in Canberra, Australia, organizational conferences were held in Bangkok, Thailand, and Bali, Indonesia, in June 1982 and November 1983, under the newly created Pacific Economic Cooperation Conference (PECC). Initially, representatives from thirteen Pacific countries attended with delegations comprised of business, academic, and government participants. Also attended by tripartite national delegations, the PECC 1982 and 1983 meetings established an international Standing Committee and five functional task forces: trade in manufactures, investment and technology transfer, agriculture and renewable resources, minerals and energy, and capital flows and finance.[6] Since Winter 1984-85, "the prospects for PECC and the Pacific process itself remained uncertain, as the business community looked for the bottom line, governments remained lukewarm, and a means for translating discussion into reality remained elusive."[7]

Formed in 1967, the Pacific Basin Economic Council (PBEC) currently maintains five business representatives from five national committees: Japan, Australia, New Zealand, the United States, and Canada. The PBEC focuses on assisting the business environment and stimulating trade and investment in the Pacific Basin. The "PBEC pursues its purposes in three principal ways. The first is to provide an international forum for an exchange of views among businessmen of the Pacific Basin and other nations on topics affecting development of the region. The second is to provide advice and counsel to governments and international agencies on basic economic and business matters affecting the Pacific Basin. The third is to provide input to other organizations concerned with Pacific development and cooperation to ensure that private sector views play a role in the contemporary dialogue about Pacific affairs."[8] PBEC emphasizes its contacts with governments and business organizations of ASEAN. According to the PBEC 1986 publication, their Pacific Region corresponds with this author's Pacific Rim Region definition minus the Soviet Union and the "Other" classification under the Pacific Island Countries heading.

Clearly politically motivated, the Asian Pacific Economic Cooperation Forum (APEC) was formed in November 1989 to facilitate trade within the region and to jointly represent their views at the Uruguay Round of multilateral trade negotiations supporting free trade throughout the world. Initiated by Australia, APEC members include Australia, New Zealand, the United States, Canada, Japan, South Korea, and ASEAN. Accounting for 40 percent of world exports and more than half of the world's gross national product, APEC anticipates that China, Hong Kong, and Taiwan will join in the near future. Starting in Punta del Este, Uruguay, in 1986, the Uruguay Round is the eighth round of negotiations to revise the General Agreements on Tariffs and Trade system. In an effort to liberalize trade and thwart protectionism, the Uruguay Round continues to deliberate to date, beyond the anticipated 7 December 1990 termination date. Compared to the previous seven rounds, where lowering tariffs was the main objective, the Uruguay Round finds itself immersed among the usual assortment of traditional items such as agricultural products to non tariff barriers, plus new areas classified as investment measures, intellectual property, and services. Even with APEC's formation 13 months before the December 1990 closing session, how effective will ASEAN and six industrial nations unite to form a common voice when each country maintains divergent agendas for the Uruguay Round? Despite particular differences, the Asian members of APEC are concerned with continued access to the western industrialized economies. Amid the rising tide of protectionism — such as the United States "Super-301" provision of the Omnibus Trade and Competitive Act of 1988 which authorizes unilateral action against unfair trading partners — Asian markets must reduce their tariff levels, liberalize their non-tariff barriers, and encourage foreign investment activity in order to alleviate reciprocating protectionism trade policies. As for the western industrialized members and Japan, intellectual property rights and anti-dumping measures are priority Uruguay Round items.

From APEC, PECC, and OPTAD to the Pacific Basin Economic Council, an inclusive Pacific Rim Region trade and economic conceptual framework remains virtually elusive among the academic, business, and government sectors. Hopefully, the practical Pacific Rim Region definition presented here will serve as a conceptual foundation when evaluating the entire Pacific Rim Region.

CHAPTER THREE

The Pacific Rim Region's Diversified International Commercial Activity

From a statistical standpoint, the Pacific Rim Region, as set forth and defined initially in this book, consists of 2.556 billion people, or 51 percent of the earth's 5.2 billion residents (Table 1). The Pacific Rim's international trade accounted for 29 percent of world trade in 1988. Compared to 1987, the Region totalled 28 percent of international trade and 27 percent in 1978. Throughout the 1978-1988 period, the Northeast Quarter's bilateral trade activity, in absolute terms, maintained its ranking position followed by the Northwest, Southwest, and Southeast Quarters. Greater than a 2 to 1 ratio in 1978, the Northwest Quarter's total trading activity increased 154 percentage points to 45 percent of the Northeast Quarter's trade value by the end of 1988. The Southwest Quarter tallied 2.3 percent of the Region's 1978 total bilateral trade with the world and 6.3 percent at yearend 1988. Since 1978, the Southeast Quarter performed 44 percent stronger by 1988. Overall, the Pacific Rim Region's aggregate international trade activity expanded almost evenly in the 1978-1988 period; importations rose by 142.20 percent while exports surged 140.80 percent. In proportion to world export and import growth, the Region's growth rates in 1978-1988 exceeded the world's international commerce expansion by 15.79 percent and 18.32 percent, respectively (Table 2).

Other than numerical computations, the Region is home to a plethora of significant economic distinctions from commodities to financial flows. Malaysia constitutes 35 percent of the world's tin output and Thailand leads the world in tin exports. Nauru, a South Pacific Island country, manages the world's largest phosphate reserve within its borders. Chile easily claims 20 percent of the global copper market and serves as the world's primary copper supplier. Also, Chile and the United States are the only countries which export raw timber in substantial quantities. Just north of Peru, Ecuador provides the largest percentage of bananas to the world marketplace. As for corn and grain production, the United States accounts for half of the world's corn production and over 20 percent of world grain output. The United States is also the world's largest agricultural exporter.

Since the 1970s, South and East Asia achieved the highest level of growth in the world, except for the oil producing nations during their

TABLE 1

Pacific Rim Region
Key Economic Indicators
1988

	Monetary Unit	Population (,000)	Literacy	Life Expectancy	Infant Mortality Rate	Area Thousands of Square Kilometers	GNP 1988 Millions US Dollars	Consumer Prices 1978-1987 Total Increases Over Prev. Yrs.
Northwest Quarter								
Soviet Union	Ruble	288,743	99%	69	25	22,402,200	2,535,300	....
Japan	Yen	123,223	99%	78	5	377,835	1,758,400	30%
North Korea	Won	22,521	95%	70	32	120,540	17,400 (1986)	....
South Korea	Won	43,347	90+%	69	24	98,480	168,950	104%
China	Renmindi Yen	1,112,299	75+%	69	34	9,596,960	372,190	44%
Taiwan	New Taiwan Dollar	20,233	94%	74	18	35,980	119,390	....
Hong Kong	Dollar	5,709	75%	76	6	1,040	54,530	87%
Philippines	Peso	64,907	88%	63	48	360,000	40,380	154%
Laos	Kip/New Kip	3,936	85%	48	128	236,800	530	....
Vietnam	Dong	66,823	78%	66	51	329,560	13,200	....
Kampuchea	Riel	6,838	48%	49	131	181,040	....	....
Thailand	Baht	55,524	82%	64	50	514,000	56,950	67%
Myanmar	Kyat	40,452	78%	54	99	678,500	257,890	56%
Malaysia	Ringgit	16,727	65%	70	31	329,750	31,110	40%
Singapore	Dollar	2,674	87%	73	9	633	24,780	33%
Brunei	Dollar	345	45%	75	10	5,770	3,300 (1986)	....
Micronesia	US Dollar	102	NA	70	26	702	1112 (1984)	....
Marshall Islands	US Dollar	42	90%	72	43	181	32 (1984)	....
Palau	US Dollar	14	NA	71	26	458	32	(GDP 1986)

TABLE 1 (continued)

Pacific Rim Region Key Economic Indicators 1988

	Monetary Unit	Population (,000)	Literacy	Life Expectancy	Infant Mortality Rate	Area Thousands of Square Kilometers	GNP 1988 Millions US Dollars	Consumer Prices 1978-1987 Total Increases Over Prev. Yrs.
Southwest Quarter								
Indonesia	Rupiah	187,651	62%	59	80	1,919,440	76,240	111%
Papau New Guinea	Kina	3,736	32%	54	97	461,690	3,320	67%
Australia	Dollar	16,452	99%	76	8	7,686,850	218,000	86%
New Zealand	Dollar	3,373	99%	75	10	268,680	23,200 (1986)	129%
Solomon Islands	Dollar	324	60%	66	41	28,450	140	97%
Fiji	Dollar	757	80%	70	19	18,270	1,020	62%
New Caledonia	CFP Franc	152	NA	70	35	19,060	....	....
Tonga	Dollar of Pa'anga	100	90-95%	71	25	748	90	....
Tuvalu	Australian Dollar	9	49±%	61	30	26	4 (1984)	....
Kiribati	Australian Dollar	69	90%	53	58	717	50	....
Vanuatu	Vatu	160	10-20%	63	37	14,760	84 (1986)	68%
Nauru	Australian Dollar	9	99%	66	41	21	130	....
Southeast Quarter								
Ecuador	Sucre	10,262	85%	65	63	283,560	9,960	....
Chile	Peso	12,827	94%	72	18	756,950	20,340	....
Western Samoa	Tala or Western Samoan Dollar	182	90%	65	48	2,860	100 (1987)	123%
French Polynesia	CFP Franc	196	NA	72	22	3,941	1,370	....
Peru	Sol	21,449	80±%	61	69	1,285,220	39,260	872%

TABLE 1 (continued)

Pacific Rim Region
Key Economic Indicators
1988

	Monetary Unit	Population (,000)	Literacy	Life Expectancy	Infant Mortality Rate	Area Thousands of Square Kilometers	GNP 1988 Millions US Dollars	Consumer Prices 1978-1987 Total Increases Over Prev. Yrs.
Northeast Quarter								
Canada	Dollar	26,311	99%	77	7	9,976,140	369,300	74%
United States	Dollar	248,231	99%	75	10	9,372,610	4,864,000	66%
Mexico	Peso	86,366	88%	69	42	1,927,550	175,200	592%
Guatemala	Quetzal	9,117	50%	62	64	108,890	7,430	118%
Honduras	Lempira	5,104	56%	64	64	112,090	4,180	78%
El Salvador	Salvadoran Colon	5,125	65%	62	62	21,040	5,620	176%
Nicaragua	Cordoba	3,503	88%	63	65	129,494	2,600 (1986)	2016%
Costa Rica	Costa Rican Colon	2,954	93%	74	17	51,100	4,530	249%
Panama	Balboa (US Dollar)	2,373	90%	72	23	78,200	4,460	43%
Colombia	Peso	31,945	88%	66	54	1,138,910	36,550	223%

Sources: International Monetary Fund. *International Financial Statistics Yearbook.* Two Editions: 1989 and 1988. Washington, D.C.

International Bank for Reconstruction and Development. *World Development Report.* Two Editions: 1988 and 1989. Washington, D.C.

Organization for Economic Cooperation and Development. *Geographic Distribution of Financial Flows.* Numerous Yearbooks: 1979/1982, 1984/1986 and 1985/1988. Paris, France.

TABLE 2

Pacific Rim Region Exports and Imports To and From the World 1978-1988, Millions of United States Dollars

Exports

	1978	1979	1980	1981	1982	1983	1984	1985	1986	1987	1988
Northwest Quarter											
Soviet Union	21,707	28,624	35,105	35,736	36,428	36,922	37,399	35,703	34,531	38,410	41,328
Japan	98,338	102,293	130,435	151,500	138,443	146,982	169,748	177,189	210,718	231,332	264,061
North Korea	892	1,103	1,182	719	778	654	691	638	673	796	931
South Korea	12,722	15,053	17,505	21,271	21,828	24,460	29,259	30,289	34,792	47,301	61,178
China	9,745	13,657	18,139	21,476	21,865	22,096	24,824	27,329	31,367	39,464	47,663
Taiwan	12,687	16,103	19,811	22,611	22,294	25,098	30,435	30,683	39,787	53,609	60,490
Hong Kong	11,498	15,160	19,724	21,796	20,996	21,949	28,314	30,182	35,438	48,473	63,166
Philippines	3,426	4,602	5,788	5,721	5,020	4,932	5,343	4,614	4807	5,696	7,034
Laos	12	17	23	17	24	27	11	18	14	66	68
Vietnam	184	158	159	152	200	235	269	332	326	413	518
Kampuchea	3	6	7	4	6	2	4	3	2	3	6
Thailand	4,086	5,301	6,501	7,027	6,946	6,368	7,414	7,123	8,864	11,564	15,992
Myanmar	234	458	453	462	398	550	526	513	505	532	588
Malaysia	7,413	11,077	12,960	11,773	12,044	14,128	16,563	15,408	13,977	17,934	21,125
Singapore	10,132	14,239	19,377	20,970	20,787	21,832	24,070	22,812	22,501	28,703	39,322
Brunei	1,845	2,653	4,589	4,001	3,258	3,367	3,183	2,934	1,798	1,805	1,987
Micronesia	....	....	....	....	....	....	2	2	2	....	....
Marshall Islands	....	3	3	3	2	3	5	3	3	....	....
Palau	....	....	....	....	....	.388	.464	.463	.464	....	....
Southwest Quarter											
Indonesia	11,643	15,579	21,909	23,810	22,329	21,146	21,881	18,597	14,809	17,170	19,376
Papua New Guinea	715	883	1,133	839	773	822	894	918	1,047	1,172	1,396
Australia	14,417	18,666	22,031	21,796	22,077	20,651	23,875	22,611	22,541	26,533	32,751
New Zealand	3,739	4,699	5,407	5,607	5,561	5,403	5,518	5,714	5,921	7,309	8,833
Solomon Islands	40	70	73	66	57	62	90	70	66	64	78

TABLE 2 (continued)

Pacific Rim Region Exports and Imports To and From the World 1978-1988, Millions of United States Dollars

Exports

	1978	1979	1980	1981	1982	1983	1984	1985	1986	1987	1988
Southwest Quarter (Continued)											
Fiji	203	259	358	311	284	240	256	230	263	281	360
New Caledonia	224	379	411	343	242	153	207	272	208	224	468
Tonga	....	....	....	9	4	5	9	5	6	7	10
Tuvalu	....	....	1	....	....	....	1	....	....	....	....
Kiribati	16	18	3	3	2	3	6	2	2	2	12
Vanuatu	33	32	20	29	15	30	43	43	26	22	33
Nauru	89	93	125	102	86	136	74	71	79	66	80
Southeast Quarter											
Ecuador	1,562	2,111	2,483	2,540	2,140	2,227	2,580	2,906	2,171	1,999	2,193
Chile	2,455	3,885	4,688	3,949	3,710	3,850	3,658	3,893	4,226	5,102	7,061
Western Samoa	10	19	17	11	13	17	20	27	10	11	15
French Polynesia	91	161	42	29	30	23	41	29	34	37	60
Peru	1,990	3,675	3,915	3,247	3,370	2,577	3,086	2,981	2,505	2,605	2,689
Northeast Quarter											
Canada	48,429	58,298	67,730	72,726	70,454	76,745	90,293	90,780	89,706	98,104	116,220
United States	143,762	182,007	220,781	233,739	212,274	200,528	217,889	213,146	217,292	252,884	320,385
Mexico	5,954	8,983	15,557	19,381	21,580	22,313	24,382	22,105	16,588	26,972	29,373
Guatemala	1,089	1,243	1,518	1,226	1,120	1,159	1,095	991	572	1,053	1,080
Honduras	602	734	829	728	668	660	766	787	906	974	949
El Salvador	845	1,223	1,070	797	876	741	718	679	735	621	689
Nicaragua	646	567	414	490	366	429	428	301	301	253	311
Costa Rica	814	934	981	1,008	871	861	986	924	1,091	1,114	1,227
Panama	257	303	350	317	308	299	251	301	332	337	287
Columbia	3,038	3,325	3,945	2,956	3,095	3,081	3,483	3,552	5,108	5,024	4,890

TABLE 2 (continued)

Pacific Rim Region Exports and Imports To and From the World 1978-1988, Millions of United States Dollars

Exports

	1978	1979	1980	1981	1982	1983	1984	1985	1986	1987	1988
TOTALS*											
Northwest Quarter	98,435	102,421	130,596	151,674	138,616	147,165	169,956	177,398	210,947	231,627	265,322
Southwest Quarter	18,169	23,382	27,462	27,428	27,662	26,076	29,416	28,345	28,479	33,761	41,606
Southeast Quarter	6,108	7,951	11,145	9,776	9,263	8,694	9,385	9,836	8,946	9,754	12,018
Northeast Quarter	192,204	240,322	288,536	306,492	282,757	277,303	308,214	303,956	307,024	351,024	436,644
Pacific Rim Region	314,916	374,076	457,739	495,370	458,298	459,238	516,971	519,535	555,396	626,166	755,590
World Trade	1,203,300	1,526,200	1,875,100	1,845,300	1,712,400	1,681,300	1,786,600	1,811,500	1,978,800	2,353,300	2,707,500

TABLE 2 (continued)

Pacific Rim Region Exports and Imports To and From the World 1978-1988, Millions of United States Dollars

Imports

	1978	1979	1980	1981	1982	1983	1984	1985	1986	1987	1988
Northwest Quarter											
Soviet Union[1]	23,293	27,965	34,628	31,935	36,492	43,894	42,489	44,308	43,019	44,719	51,585
Japan	79,900	109,833	141,284	142,862	131,566	126,520	136,142	130,516	127,660	150,907	187,483
North Korea[1]	659	903	1,128	928	922	969	813	825	839	1,120	1,230
South Korea	14,976	20,350	22,289	26,155	24,250	26,196	30,628	31,058	31,734	41,025	51,433
China	10,915	15,675	19,505	21,631	18,920	21,313	25,953	42,480	43,247	43,222	55,352
Taiwan	11,026	14,774	19,734	21,200	18,888	20,334	21,999	20,123	24,160	34,590	49,582
Hong Kong	13,449	17,139	22,403	24,694	23,544	24,005	28,558	29,701	35,360	48,463	63,990
Philippines	5,143	6,613	8,295	8,477	8,262	7,863	6,262	5,351	5,211	6,937	8,662
Laos	71	84	123	85	88	93	50	65	70	100	132
Vietnam	1,019	973	996	811	637	489	593	645	631	663	804
Kampuchea	21	29	155	79	55	60	53	33	17	17	26
Thailand	5,355	7,164	9,213	9,954	8,547	10,283	10,415	9,260	9,166	13,003	16,292
Myanmar	326	332	657	764	846	721	623	656	670	660	741
Malaysia	5,929	7,842	10,821	11,581	12,409	13,241	14,057	12,301	10,826	12,701	16,567
Singapore	13,061	17,643	24,013	27,571	28,176	28,158	28,667	26,237	25,513	32,626	43,869
Brunei	281	396	573	589	899	724	622	606	653	1,230	1,256
Micronesia	....	....	....	....	....	....	37	40	44	....	....
Marshall Islands	....	14	17	22	20	18	23	29	29	....	....
Palau	....	....	....	....	....	14	25	22	25	....	....
Southwest Quarter											
Indonesia	6,690	7,226	10,837	13,270	16,859	16,351	13,880	10,275	10,724	12,850	13,489
Papua New Guinea	708	877	1,062	1,152	1,171	1,121	972	906	971	1,211	1,512
Australia	15,577	18,309	22,491	26,210	26,552	21,478	25,929	25,896	26,056	29,353	36,068
New Zealand	3,489	4,553	5,472	5,739	5,793	5,334	6,144	5,943	5,997	7,263	7,378
Solomon Islands	45	71	91	99	69	74	79	83	72	81	125

TABLE 2 **(continued)**

Pacific Rim Region Exports and Imports To and From the World 1978-1988, Millions of United States Dollars

Imports

	1978	1979	1980	1981	1982	1983	1984	1985	1986	1987	1988
Southwest Quarter (Continued)											
Fiji	356	470	559	631	509	484	450	441	398	309	441
New Caledonia	311	386	506	408	367	304	310	347	531	624	604
Tonga	....	....	....	40	42	38	41	41	40	48	66
Tuvalu	....	....	2	4	6	3	4	4	4	5	4
Kiribati	18	17	25	37	43	23	18	16	19	17	24
Vanuatu	56	53	43	39	38	64	62	66	69	95	221
Nauru	27	23	32	30	26	33	22	33	29	32	28
Southeast Quarter											
Ecuador	1,505	1,600	2,254	2,246	1,985	1,465	1,767	1,857	1,811	2,229	1,714
Chile	3,002	4,218	5,124	6,364	3,536	2,968	3,481	3,079	3,132	4,024	5,074
Western Samoa	54	71	63	67	50	48	68	51	48	68	98
French Polynesia	259	295	278	267	269	372	324	310	488	521	614
Peru	1,459	1,903	2,950	3,880	4,126	2,442	1,791	1,709	2,089	3,682	2,531
Northeast Quarter											
Canada	46,388	59,966	62,834	70,030	58,418	64,808	77,750	80,640	85,391	92,700	111,600
United States	186,050	222,355	256,959	273,351	254,882	269,880	341,170	361,620	387,075	424,068	459,910
Mexico	7,560	12,086	19,456	24,126	15,039	8,635	10,812	13,992	12,898	20,888	28,841
Guatemala	1,286	1,504	1,598	1,673	1,388	1,135	1,448	1,297	1,156	1,314	1,512
Honduras	699	826	1,005	945	692	820	937	827	818	848	926
El Salvador	1,031	1,040	971	981	955	892	977	961	912	1,091	1,257
Nicaragua	593	360	882	804	690	747	665	544	466	494	540
Costa Rica	1,092	1,398	1,471	1,209	893	990	1,091	1,097	1,145	1,385	1,409
Panama	942	1,184	1,492	1,556	1,582	1,412	1,423	1,391	1,285	1,306	3,151
Columbia	2,836	3,233	4,663	5,199	5,478	4,968	4,492	4,131	3,931	4,227	5,030

TABLE 2 (continued)

Pacific Rim Region Exports and Imports To and From the World 1978-1988, Millions of United States Dollars

Imports

	1978	1979	1980	1981	1982	1983	1984	1985	1986	1987	1988
TOTALS*											
Northwest Quarter	80,006	109,971	141,477	143,060	131,749	126,718	136,354	130,740	127,891	151,186	187,844
Southwest Quarter	19,074	22,871	27,976	31,965	32,364	26,830	32,089	44,063	32,066	36,631	43,463
Southeast Quarter	6,279	8,087	10,669	12,824	9,966	7,295	5,841	7,006	7,568	10,524	10,031
Northeast Quarter	232,454	282,323	319,851	343,417	313,327	334,708	418,942	442,284	472,489	516,800	571,553
Pacific Rim Region	337,813	423,252	499,973	531,266	487,406	495,551	593,226	624,093	647,582	715,141	812,891
World Trade	1,247,600	1,569,100	1,928,700	1,912,300	1,798,700	1,738,500	1,849,700	1,890,300	2,063,600	2,433,000	2,793,100

Note: Exports figures are presented free-on-board (f.o.b.), and imports are presented inclusive of cost, insurance, and freight (c.i.f.), unless noted differently.

[1] Minus insurance and freight.

* Due to rounding of some individual Quarter member subtotals, total figures will vary from the actual total.

Sources: International Monetary Fund. *Direction of Trade Statistics Yearbook*. Various Issues: 1984, 1988 and 1989.

peak price periods.[9] As mentioned earlier, trans-Pacific trade exceeded trans-Atlantic trade in 1982, and by 1990 trans-Pacific trade will double trans-Atlantic commerce figures. According to some observers, intra-Asian trade will surpass trans-Pacific trade by the early 1990s.[10] Utilizing cheap labor, and open access to the developed world, Japan and Hong Kong, followed by Taiwan and South Korea, built the foundations of their successful export led economies through the garment industry during the 1960s and 1970s. Thanks to the textile-quota system stipulated in the Multifiber Agreement (MFA), Hong Kong, South Korea, Taiwan, and China still maintain their positions as the dominant, cheap garment suppliers to the United States. According to the World Bank and the *Far Eastern Economic Review*, these four exporters supplied 49 percent of total United States apparel and textile imports totalling $12.9 billion. Through the MFA textile-quota system, receipts totalled $200 billion due to specified market exposure in the United States and the European Communities.[11]

Also benefitting from export-led growth are the newly industrializing economies (NIEs) or the newly industrializing countries (NICs). Depending on the information source, variations of the "newly industrializing" category vary. The International Monetary Fund (IMF) classifies South Korea, Singapore, Taiwan, and Hong Kong as the NIEs. Within the international business community, NIEs are also referred to as "the four tigers" or "the four dragons." In some instances, a reference to the NICs will appear — again, depending on the source — which usually connotes the NIEs plus Malaysia, Thailand, and Indonesia. Whatever the classification, each of these seven economies continues to experience phenomenal growth. In 1989 alone, save Hong Kong's GDP figure due to the 1997 merger date with mainland China, consider these GDP growth rates: South Korea, 6.3 percent; Singapore, 9.2 percent; Taiwan, 7.7 percent; Hong Kong, 2.5 percent; Malaysia, 8.5 percent; Thailand, 12.2 percent; and Indonesia, 6.2 percent.[12]

Singapore, South Korea, and Taiwan maintained export/import growth levels within the 70 percent to 79 percent range from 1978 to 1988. Hong Kong surpassed 80 percent growth of exports from 1978 to 1988 while imports followed close at 79 percent. Malaysia's export/import growth from 1978 to 1988 hovered around 64 percent while Thailand's exports registered at a 74 percent increase and imports rose 67 percent in the same period. Indonesia, the only newly industrialized Asian economy in the Southwestern Quarter, showed modest international trade growth from 1978 to 1988: exports grew 40 percent and imports by 50 percent (Table 3). Malaysia, Thailand, and Indonesia are endowed with natural resources. One common feature to each concerns tin; Malaysia is the largest tin producer, Thailand is the largest exporter, and Indonesia ranks as a major producer of tin. Malaysia also produces rubber, palm oil, along with oil and gas. Known as the rice bowl of Asia, Thailand's distinction as one of the leading net exporters of food coincides with quantity, in terms of production, rather than with efficient production methods. Indonesia's economy generates 50 percent of its export earnings from oil and gas. As a major producer of tin, nickel ores, and bauxite, Indonesia's mining sector, as with Malaysia and Thailand, enjoyed the later 1980s price levels. By late 1989, demand levels fell with steep declines: nickel, 43 percent; aluminum, 34 percent; and copper, 31 percent.[13] Prices rebounded by early 1990 but were well below early 1989 levels. Fueled by the garment industry, electronics manufacturing, commerce, small manufactures, agriculture, mining, along with increasing levels of Japanese direct investment and aid, these "newly industrializing" Asian economies clearly benefit from favorable trade policies in the western industrialized nations and Japan.

Within the Region, Japan, Australia, and the United States contribute substantial Official Development Assistance (ODA) to developing countries. As members of the OECD's eighteen-member Development Assistance Committee (DAC), Japan, Australia, and the United States accounted for 75 percent of DAC's ODA 1988 total (Table 4). According to the OECD, Japan surpassed the United States as the largest donor in 1989. Japan's ratio of aid to GNP remained at 0.32 percent in 1989, where the United States ratio fell from 0.21 to 0.15 percent.[14] These GNP percentage comparisons can be deceiving since the United States GNP is almost twice that of Japan's. Official Development Assistance, as defined by the Development Assistance Committee, "are those flows to developing countries and multilateral institutions provided by official agencies, including state and local governments, or their executive agencies, each transaction of which meets the following tests:

a) It is administered with the promotion of the economic development and welfare of development countries as its main objective, and

b) It is concessional in character and contains a 'grant element' of at least 25 percent."[15]

TABLE 3

Percentage Change of Exports and Imports from 1978 to 1988 and Economic Resources by Country

	% Change of Exports From 1978 to 1988	% Change of Imports From 1978 to 1988	Economic Resources	
Northwest Quarter				
Soviet Union	90	121	Agricultural:	Grain, cotton, sugar beets, potatoes, vegetables, sunflowers
			Manufactures:	Steel, machinery, vehicles, chemicals, textiles, paper
			Minerals:	Iron, manganese, antimony, bauxite, molybdenum, oil, potassium salts
Japan	169	135	Agricultural:	Rice, grains, vegetables, fruits
			Manufactures:	Electrical and electronic equipment, automobiles, chemicals
			Minerals:	Sulfur, limestone, molybdenum, manganese, zinc, copper, coal
North Korea	4	87	Agricultural:	Corn, potatoes, fruits, vegetables, rice
			Manufactures:	Textiles, petrochemicals, food processing
			Minerals:	Coal, lead tungsten, graphite, magnetite, fluorspar
South Korea	381	243	Agricultural:	Rice, barley, vegetables, wheat
			Manufactures:	Electronics, ships, textiles, clothing, motor vehicles
			Minerals:	Tungsten, coal, graphite
China	389	407	Agricultural:	Grain, rice, cotton, tea
			Manufactures:	Iron, steel, textiles, agricultural implements, trucks
			Minerals:	Tungsten, antimony, coal, manganese, tin, molybdenum
Taiwan	377	350	Agricultural:	Rice, bananas, pineapples, sugar cane, peanuts, sweet potatoes
			Manufactures:	Textiles, clothing, electronics, chemicals, plastics, processed foods
			Minerals:	Coal, limestone, marble

TABLE 3 (continued)

Percentage Change of Exports and Imports from 1978 to 1988 and Economic Resources by Country

	% Change of Exports From 1978 to 1988	% Change of Imports From 1978 to 1988	Economic Resources	
Northwest Quarter (continued)				
Hong Kong	449	376	Agricultural:	Rice, sweet potatoes, yams, taro, Chinese kale
			Manufactures:	Textiles, apparel, shipbuilding, small manufacturers, electronics, fish products
			Minerals:	Feldspar, kaolin
Philippines	105	68	Agricultural:	Sugar, rice, corn, pineapple, coconut
			Manufactures:	Food processing, textiles, clothing, drugs, wood products
			Minerals:	Cobalt, copper, gold, nickel, silver, iron, petroleum
Laos	466	86	Agricultural:	Rice, corn, tobacco, opium, cotton, citrus fruits, coffee
			Manufactures:	Wood products
			Minerals:	Tin
Vietnam	182	-21	Agricultural:	Rice, rubber, corn, manioc, sugar cane
			Manufactures:	Textiles, cement, food processing, chemical fertilizers, steel
			Minerals:	Coal, iron, phosphates, manganese, bauxite, apatite, chromate
Kampuchea	100	24	Agricultural:	Rice, sugar, kapok
			Manufactures:	Rice milling, wood, rubber
			Minerals:	Iron, copper, manganese
Thailand	291	204	Agricultural:	Rice, corn, tapioca, sugar cane
			Manufactures:	Textiles, mining, wood products
			Minerals:	Antimony, tin, tungsten, iron, gas

TABLE 3 (continued)

Percentage Change of Exports and Imports from 1978 to 1988 and Economic Resources by Country

	% Change of Exports From 1978 to 1988	% Change of Imports From 1978 to 1988	Economic Resources	
Northwest Quarter (continued)				
Myanmar	151	127	Agricultural:	Rice, sugar cane, peanuts, beans
			Manufactures:	Rubber
			Minerals:	Oil, lead, silver, tin, tungsten, precious stones
Malaysia	185	179	Agricultural:	Palm oil, coconut, rice, pepper
			Manufactures:	Rubber goods, steel, electronics
			Minerals:	Tin, iron
Singapore	288	236	Agricultural:	Vegetables, eggs
			Manufactures:	Shipbuilding, rubber, lumber processing, oil refining, electronics, textiles.
			Minerals:	
Brunei	8	347	Agricultural:	Rice, bananas, cassava
			Manufactures:	Petroleum
			Minerals:	Oil
Micronesia	....	....	Agricultural:	Coconuts, taro, breadfruit, yams, poultry
			Manufactures:	Bottling, handicrafts, bakeries, boatbuilding
			Minerals:	Due to land shortage, exploitation is negligible
Marshall Islands	....	....	Agricultural:	Coconuts, taros, breadfruit, vegetables, poultry
			Manufactures:	Handicrafts, fish processing, bakeries, boat building
			Other Resources:	Commercial fishing
Palau	....	....	Agricultural:	Coconut, cassava, sweet potatoes
			Manufactures:	Craft items (shell, wood, pearl)
			Other Resources:	Commercial Fishing

TABLE 3 (continued)

Percentage Change of Exports and Imports from 1978 to 1988 and Economic Resources by Country

	% Change of Exports From 1978 to 1988	% Change of Imports From 1978 to 1988		Economic Resources
Southwest Quarter				
Indonesia	66	102	Agricultural:	Rice, coffee, sugar
			Manufactures:	Food processing, textiles, light industry, rubber
			Minerals:	Nickel, tin, oil, bauxite, copper, natural gas
Papau New Guinea	95	114	Agricultural:	Coffee, coconuts, cocoa
			Manufactures:	Negligible
			Minerals:	Gold, copper, silver, gas
Australia	127	132	Agricultural:	Wheat, barley, oats, corn, sugar, vegetables
			Manufactures:	Iron, steel, textiles, electrical equipment, chemicals, aircraft
			Minerals:	Coal, copper, iron, lead, tin, uranium, zinc
New Zealand	136	111	Agricultural:	Grain
			Manufactures:	Food processing, textiles, machinery, fish products, forest products
			Minerals:	Oil, gas, iron, coal
Solomon Islands	95	177	Agricultural:	Coconuts, rice, bananas, yams
			Manufactures:	Fish canning
			Other Resources:	Forests, marine shell
Fiji	77	24	Agricultural:	Sugar, bananas, ginger
			Manufactures:	Sugar, light industry
			Minerals:	Gold

TABLE 3 (continued)

Percentage Change of Exports and Imports from 1978 to 1988 and Economic Resources by Country

	% Change of Exports From 1978 to 1988	% Change of Imports From 1978 to 1988	Economic Resources	
Southwest Quarter (continued)				
New Caledonia	109	94	Agricultural:	Coffee, coconut, cotton, manioc, corn, tobacco, bananas, pineapple
			Manufactures:	Copra
			Minerals:	Nickel, chrome, iron, cobalt, manganese, gold, copper, silver, lead
Tonga	....	....	Agricultural:	Manioc, tomatoes, oranges, capsicum, livestock
			Manufactures:	Coconut oil, desiccated coconut, copra, leather, paint products
			Minerals:	Copper, zinc
Tuvalu	....	....	Agricultural:	Polaka, taro, bananas, coconuts
			Manufactures:	Postage stamps, copra, baking, construction
			Other Resources:	Commercial fishing
Kiribati	-25	33	Agricultural:	Coconut, breadfruit, pandanus, bananas, paw-paw
			Manufactures:	Copra
			Other Resources:	Commercial fishing
Vanuatu	0	295	Agricultural:	Coconut, cocoa, coffee, cattle
			Manufactures:	Frozen fish, canned meat
			Minerals:	Manganese
Nauru	-10	4	Agricultural:	Coconuts, pandanos, vegetables, livestock
			Manufactures:	Phosphate processing
			Other Resources:	Phosphate mining

TABLE 3 (continued)

Percentage Change of Exports and Imports from 1978 to 1988 and Economic Resources by Country

	% Change of Exports From 1978 to 1988	% Change of Imports From 1978 to 1988	Economic Resources	
Southeast Quarter				
Ecuador	40	14	Agricultural:	Bananas, coffee, rice, sugar, corn
			Manufactures:	Food processing, wood products, textiles
			Minerals:	Oil, copper, iron, lead, silver, sulphur
Chile	188	69	Agricultural:	Grain, onions, beans, potatoes, peas, fruits, grapes
			Manufactures:	Steel, textiles, wood products
			Minerals:	Copper, molybdenum, nitrates, iodine, iron, coal, oil, manganese, mica, sulphur, marble, onyx
Western Samoa	50	81	Agricultural:	Cocoa, coconut, bananas
			Manufactures:	Copra
			Other Resources:	Hardwoods, fish
French Polynesia	-34	137	Agricultural:	Coconuts, vanilla, mother-of-pearl shells, culture, pearls, coffee
			Manufactures:	Coconut oil, coconut meal, soap, monoi (scented coconut oil)
			Other Resources:	Tourism, breweries, fruit juice factories, power station
Peru	35	73	Agricultural:	Cotton, sugar, coffee, corn
			Manufactures:	Fish meal, mineral processing, light industry, textiles
			Minerals:	Copper, lead, molybdenum, silver, zinc, iron, oil

TABLE 3 (continued)

Percentage Change of Exports and Imports from 1978 to 1988 and Economic Resources by Country

	% Change of Exports From 1978 to 1988	% Change of Imports From 1978 to 1988	Economic Resources	
Northeast Quarter				
Canada	140	141	Agricultural:	Livestock, grains, dairy products, food processing, oil, seeds, tobacco
			Manufactures:	Transportation equipment, processed and unprocessed minerals, food products, wood products, petroleum and natural gas
			Minerals:	Nickel, zinc, copper, gold, molybdenum, silver
United States	123	147	Agricultural:	Corn, soybean, wheat, cotton
			Manufactures:	Transportation equipment, electronics, petroleum
			Minerals:	Coal, oil, bauxite, steel, aerospace, telecommunications, food processing, consumer goods
Mexico	393	281	Agricultural:	Cotton, coffee, sugar cane, vegetables, corn,
			Manufactures:	Steel, chemicals, petroleum, electric goods, textiles
			Minerals:	Silver, lead, zinc, gold, oil, natural gas
Guatemala	-1	18	Agricultural:	Coffee, sugar, bananas, cotton, corn
			Manufactures:	Prepared goods, textiles, tires
			Minerals:	Oil, nickel
Honduras	58	32	Agricultural:	Bananas, coffee, corn, beans
			Manufactures:	Clothing, textiles, cement, wood products, cigars
			Minerals:	Gold, silver, copper, lead, zinc, iron, antimony, coal
El Salvador	-18	22	Agricultural:	Coffee, cotton, corn, sugar
			Manufactures:	Food, beverages, textiles, petroleum products
			Other Resources:	Rubber, timber

TABLE 3 (continued)

Percentage Change of Exports and Imports from 1978 to 1988 and Economic Resources by Country

	% Change of Exports From 1978 to 1988	% Change of Imports From 1978 to 1988	Economic Resources	
Northeast Quarter (continued)				
Nicaragua	-52	-9	Agricultural:	Bananas, cotton, fruit, yucca, coffee, sugar, corn, beans, cocoa, rice, sesame, tobacco
			Manufactures:	Oil refining, food processing, chemicals, textiles
			Minerals:	Gold, silver, copper, tungsten
Costa Rica	51	29	Agricultural:	Coffee, bananas, sugar, cocoa, cotton, hemp
			Manufactures:	Fiberglass, aluminum, textiles, fertilizers, roofing, cement
			Minerals:	Gold, salt, sulphur, iron
Panama	12	235	Agricultural:	Bananas, pineapples, cocoa, corn, coconuts, sugar
			Manufactures:	Oil refining
			Minerals:	Copper
Colombia	61	77	Agricultural:	Coffee, rice, corn, cotton, sugar, bananas
			Manufactures:	Textiles, processed goods, hides, steel, cement, chemicals
			Minerals:	Oil, gas, emeralds, gold, copper, lead, coal, iron, nickel, salt

TABLE 3 (continued)

Percentage Change of Exports and Imports from 1978 to 1988 and Economic Resources by Country

Aggregate Percentages	Total % Change in Exports From 1978 to 1988	Total % Change in Imports From 1978 to 1988
Pacific Rim Region	140.80	142.20
World	125.01	123.88

Sources: Paxton, John. Editor. *The Statesman's Yearbook 1989-90*. 126th Edition. New York: St. Martin's Press, 1989.

International Monetary Fund. *Direction of Trade Statistics Yearbook*. Various Issues: 1984, 1988 and 1989.

TABLE 4

Foreign Aid by Development Assistance Committee (DAC) Countries, Actual Amounts Disbursed 1979 - 1988 Millions of United States Dollars

Total Official Gross	1979	1980	1981	1982	1983	1984	1985	1987	1987	1988
Australia	499.6	512.8	587.4	654.3	652.9	684.6	560.0	553.5	560.7	692.0
Austria	63.6	153.5	264.8	169.6	136.5	156.3	200.7	228.4	285.1	295.1
Belgium	495.1	658.0	445.8	434.8	391.1	489.2	397.0	439.0	785.5	722.9
Canada	1,632.0	2,171.4	1,217.6	1,641.9	1,535.6	1,703.8	1,536.4	1,509.0	1,845.9	2,200.8
Denmark	364.7	292.5	328.7	317.4	417.2	418.8	397.9	548.6	575.3	534.8
Finland	85.8	66.4	78.6	86.6	93.0	108.7	128.0	187.9	263.0	382.4
France	3,750.1	4,719.4	4,434.9	4,014.3	3,873.6	4,735.6	4,885.2	5,821.2	8,250.6	7,405.5
Germany, F.R.	3,593.4	4,662.4	3,775.3	3,537.3	3,475.2	3,589.2	3,945.2	5,333.3	6,252.7	7,431.2
Ireland	....	....	....	12.2	14.0	14.6	17.2	25.3	27.3	203.5
Italy	375.4	544.7	692.8	811.8	810.1	1,138.3	1,534.6	2,175.6	3,271.4	2,854.2
Japan	2,729.6	3,032.2	3,108.0	3,494.2	3,946.6	3,833.8	3,641.1	5,682.4	8,423.6	10,165.2
Netherlands	1,124.7	1,344.1	1,196.3	1,122.6	903.1	934.6	850.7	1,280.9	1,557.1	1,714.5
New Zealand	56.9	56.7	51.7	50.5	48.8	44.8	44.0	61.7	66.8	94.0
Norway	259.1	286.3	266.7	349.1	351.8	304.4	345.2	480.7	529.9	576.3
Sweden	650.9	715.1	603.8	968.6	919.5	894.8	1020.5	1348.5	900.1	1089.3
Switzerland	177.7	189.9	182.7	198.4	252.9	221.7	229.4	327.6	391.9	488.6
United Kingdom	1,837.1	2,212.2	2,385.8	1,816.8	1,451.7	1,412.6	1,446.6	1,517.0	1,469.8	1,950.6
United States	7,040.00	7,771.0	7,654.0	8,867.0	8,773.0	10,155.0	11,327.0	10,423.0	9,667.0	11,340.0
Total	**24,735.5**	**29,388.5**	**27,274.9**	**28,547.4**	**28,046.5**	**30,840.8**	**21,450.7**	**24,575.9**	**26,706.3**	**29,788.7**

Source: Organization for Economic Cooperation and Development. *Geographic Distribution of Financial Flows*. Numerous Yearbooks: 1979/1982, 1984/1986, and 1985/1988. Paris, France.

Since the current accepted market rate for a loan is 10 percent, the grant element for a 10 percent loan is nil. As for a grant, the grant element is 100 percent. Within these parameters, this type of funding is referred to as a soft loan. "Generally speaking, a loan will not convey a grant element of over 25 percent if its maturity is less than 10 years, unless its interest rate is well below 3 percent. If the face value of a loan is multiplied by its grant element, the result is referred to as the grant element of that loan."[16]

Due to Japan's economic prominence within the Northwest Quarter, and as the second largest GNP producer, Japan has evolved as the home to the world's ten wealthiest banks in terms of assets. Accompanied with the liberalization of its financial markets, Asian manufactures target Japan, while nations such as South Korea, Thailand, and Taiwan are maintaining a growing percentage of yen as foreign currency reserve.[17] With Japan in mind, it is the first of the following four evaluations of the predominant economy in each Quarter to be considered in Chapter Four.

CHAPTER FOUR

The Economic Context, Trade Policies, Exchange Arrangements/Exchange Restrictions, and Major Investment Trends in Each of the Four Predominant Economies

Japan - The Economic Context and Trade Policy

Emerging from the Second World War as a defeated, imperialistic empire, Japan's economic development concentrated on rebuilding the predominantly destroyed infrastructure, generating income, and re-establishing domestic and international business contacts. Export earnings served, and continue to serve, as the focus of economic policy to enhance economic growth. By 1964, Japan's positive trade balance reflected effective economic planning and trade policies when considering a devastated Japanese economy 19 years prior. Thanks to United States funding, as with West Germany, Japan's post-war economic development proved profitable in terms of economic growth for United States manufacturing interests, as well as for rebuilding Japan's economy and infrastructure. In fact, due to Japan's ardent efficiency, Japanese electronics, automobiles, and business savvy elevated Japan's economy to the world's second leading industrial nation status with respect to output. In terms of financial strength, Japan is perhaps the strongest on paper due to: exceptional automobile and electronic export receipts during the 1980s, pervasive trade protection, a high per capita savings rate, and a lucrative stock market where 40-50 percent price/earnings ratios far exceed the 11 to 17 percent price/earnings ratios in the other industrialized nations.

In terms of international trade during 1978-1988, Japan's major export manufactures were automobiles, iron and steel, office machines, optical equipment, and watches, plus tape recorders and videotape records. Petroleum, fish and fish products, liquified natural gas, coal, and lumber are primary Japanese imports. Throughout the post-war period, the United States continues to be Japan's leading trade partner. On a bilateral comparison, in proportion to United States trade with Japan, in November 1989, the combined Asian trade with Japan exceeded Japan's trade activity with the United States for the first time. Other major Japanese export partners are West Germany, South Korea and Taiwan. Major suppliers include South Korea, Australia, and Taiwan. Since 1978 to 1988, Japanese imports increased 135 percent, whereas Japanese exports expanded 169 percent in the same period. With the September 1985 to June 1988 yen appreciation vis-à-vis the United States dollar, from 240 yen to 125 yen/$1, Japanese export activity, denominated in yen, actually declined by 8,641 billion yen during the 1985-1987 period where imports declined 9,348 billion yen. In the Pacific Rim Region framework, the United States is clearly Japan's largest bilateral trading partner. South Korea, Hong Kong, the People's Republic of China, Singapore, and Australia follow at a considerable distance in purchases from Japan. In comparison, Japanese exports to the United States surpassed South Korean bound exports, in 1988, by $74.8 billion. As for supplier markets, other than the United States, South Korea ranks as the leading point of origin location in 1988, followed by Australia, the People's Republic of China, Indonesia, and Canada (Table 5).

Exceptionally deficient in vital natural resources integral to current Japanese industrial production and domestic consumption (for example: oil, natural gas, steel, and timber), Japan's economic prosperity is most vulnerable to world commodity price fluctuations and natural resource availabilities among trading partners (Table 6). Also, with an aging population, deficient health services, and an ailing transportation infrastructure, Japan's high savings rate and strong cash position will inevitably be redirected in the decades ahead.

Due to external influences, particularly the United States, Japan's "establishment of a state on the basis of foreign trade" objective is shifting to some degree. Shifting, in the sense, that economic growth would depend more on domestic demand amid sluggish export figures since 1986. Contributing to this trend is the yen's appreciation from 240 yen/$1 in September 1985 to approximately 125 yen/$1 in June 1988; and a very restricted domestic market with respect to imports from Japan's largest trading partner, the United States. Representing goods, services, and sales among international transactions, Japan's current account position reached a record level of $87 billion in 1987 along with the fifth consecutive positive trade balance level from $31.46 billion to $96.46 billion in 1983 and 1987.

TABLE 5

Japan's Bilateral Trade with Pacific Rim Region, Selected Members 1978-1988
Millions of United States Dollars

Exports

	1978	1979	1980	1981	1982	1983	1984	1985	1986	1987	1988
Northwest Quarter											
Soviet Union	2,529	2,443	2,796	3,253	3,893	2,822	2,515	2,772	3,178	2,587	3,131
North Korea	185	281	376	290	313	328	254	249	185	216	239
South Korea	6,056	6,201	5,393	5,640	4,869	6,006	7,211	7,159	10,557	13,344	15,442
China, People's Republic	3,074	3,674	5,109	5,076	3,500	4,918	7,199	12,590	9,936	8,337	9,486
Taiwan	3,673	4,558	5,320	5,920	4,780	5,088	5,976	5,068	7,902	11,449	14,357
Hong Kong	3,112	3,652	4,784	5,292	4,707	5,291	6,546	6,564	7,215	8,947	11,708
Philippines	1,559	1,610	1,692	1,924	1,799	1,744	1,072	946	1,098	1,429	1,740
Laos	5	9	13	9	10	15	5	12	13	16	20
Vietnam	218	117	114	109	92	119	119	150	190	181	194
Kampuchea	....	1	26	10	5	3	5	2	2	1	5
Thailand	1,541	1,701	1,925	2,243	1,903	2,508	2,420	2,047	2,045	2,982	5,164
Myanmar	232	251	215	249	231	179	181	186	213	178	184
Malaysia	1,168	1,496	2,070	2,416	2,496	2,772	2,869	2,184	1,723	2,188	3,061
Singapore	2,345	2,660	3,929	4,454	4,357	4,449	4,602	3,893	4,611	6,063	8,312
Brunei	51	75	89	93	144	86	72	91	59	41	67
Southwest Quarter											
Indonesia	2,114	2,110	3,476	4,115	4,251	3,552	3,067	2,191	2,682	3,017	3,055
Papua New Guinea	112	122	168	178	127	142	141	135	139	182	209
Australia	2,718	2,587	3,407	4,768	4,561	4,283	5,173	5,430	5,273	5,196	6,684
New Zealand	422	581	680	910	925	965	1,160	1,082	1,113	1,137	1,039
Solomon Islands	5	10	13	9	8	15	15	16	20	18	17
Fiji	47	51	62	71	53	57	53	50	44	30	31
New Caledonia	10	13	18	14	18	12	12	8	18	21	22
Tonga	3	2	1	3	1	....	....	....	....	....	....

TABLE 5 (continued)

Japan's Bilateral Trade with Pacific Rim Region, Selected Members 1978-1988
Millions of United States Dollars

Exports

	1978	1979	1980	1981	1982	1983	1984	1985	1986	1987	1988
Southwest Quarter (continued)											
Tuvalu	....	....	....	....	2	3	3	2	4	3	4
Vanuatu	6	10	5	5	5	8	7	7	14	11	35
Nauru	2	3	3	5	2	1	4	1	1	....	....
Southeast Quarter											
Ecuador	186	201	276	293	218	92	122	176	274	220	116
Peru	95	141	307	350	322	181	160	142	226	219	119
Chile	227	244	464	738	231	141	290	170	297	355	368
Western Samoa	8	5	4	5	5	4	6	7	4	6	8
French Polynesia	9	10	17	13	14	15	17	17	25	29	24
Northeast Quarter											
Canada	1,888	1,725	2,449	3,387	2,851	3,625	4,286	4,559	5,571	5,661	6,426
United States	25,362	26,452	31,910	38,883	36,546	43,339	60,429	66,684	81,926	85,017	90,245
Mexico	644	835	1,228	1,699	974	579	886	1,004	1,041	1,402	1,773
Guatemala	114	109	112	105	47	44	59	51	46	79	73
Honduras	53	54	84	46	36	39	37	47	71	66	72
El Salvador	109	70	31	30	24	31	40	44	33	60	41
Nicaragua	27	7	20	12	9	9	13	24	9	14	13
Costa Rica	137	145	144	69	27	44	72	86	100	106	60
Panama	1,467	890	1,427	2,204	2,918	2,174	3,453	3,357	3,224	2,440	2,660
Colombia	295	360	500	496	595	456	403	428	389	392	527

TABLE 5 (continued)

Japan's Bilateral Trade with Pacific Rim Region, Selected Members 1978-1988
Millions of United States Dollars

Imports

	1978	1979	1980	1981	1982	1983	1984	1985	1986	1987	1988
Northwest Quarter											
Soviet Union	1,453	1,895	1,873	2,020	1,668	1,458	1,388	1,438	1,988	2,368	2,772
North Korea	108	151	181	140	151	127	144	177	170	240	323
South Korea	2,630	3,358	3,040	3,395	3,270	3,407	4,205	4,144	5,334	8,173	11,827
China, People's Republic	2,045	2,933	4,346	5,283	5,338	5,089	5,943	6,534	5,727	7,478	9,861
Taiwan	1,570	2,248	2,173	2,454	2,369	2,619	3,197	3,416	4,720	7,198	8,739
Hong Kong	501	658	573	668	621	671	839	774	1,080	1,578	2,111
Philippines	1,066	1,570	1,964	1,712	1,570	1,305	1,414	1,252	1,235	1,375	2,048
Laos	4	9	6	4	1	3	1	1	1	2	7
Vietnam	51	48	49	37	36	38	51	66	84	145	196
Kampuchea	....	1	....	1	1	....	....	....	....	1	1
Thailand	849	1,160	1,125	1,058	1,036	1,019	1,037	1,035	1,401	1,815	2,754
Myanmar	51	88	77	63	49	47	32	35	49	35	32
Malaysia	1,911	3,232	3,504	2,917	3,000	3,125	4,402	4,347	3,986	4,814	4,741
Singapore	878	1,461	1,516	1,938	1,821	1,468	1,773	1,607	1,475	2,081	2,338
Brunei	1,403	1,878	3,263	2,896	2,630	2,383	2,197	1,906	1,302	1,193	1,134
Southwest Quarter											
Indonesia	5,284	8,725	13,230	13,263	11,955	10,441	11,141	10,192	7,386	8,499	9,606
Papua New Guinea	229	364	407	327	285	322	283	253	297	403	568
Australia	5,340	6,248	7,018	7,404	6,935	6,644	7,278	7,516	7,046	7,973	10,285
New Zealand	644	800	834	883	856	930	933	910	964	1,178	1,645
Solomon Islands	11	21	28	34	43	35	42	44	31	30	32
Fiji	2	4	33	36	6	8	8	11	19	41	25
New Caledonia	60	100	138	112	88	61	65	78	48	52	159
Tonga	....	....	....	....	....	....	....	....	....	....	1

TABLE 5 (continued)

Japan's Bilateral Trade with Pacific Rim Region, Selected Members 1978-1988
Millions of United States Dollars

Imports

	1978	1979	1980	1981	1982	1983	1984	1985	1986	1987	1988
Southwest Quarter (continued)											
Tuvalu	....	....	....	....	....	....	....	....	....	....	....
Vanuatu	2	2	1	....	....	1	4	4	2	4	3
Nauru	5	7	10	5	2	4	1	....	....	....	....
Southeast Quarter											
Ecuador	25	36	257	407	24	26	23	48	78	71	84
Peru	301	507	477	601	541	487	406	334	329	328	413
Chile	370	545	648	530	577	503	635	538	540	623	1,022
Western Samoa	1	1	1	2	4	1	1	....	1	1	1
French Polynesia	4	3	2	4	3	2	9	10	11	17	27
Northeast Quarter											
Canada	3,206	4,074	4,752	4,449	4,426	4,428	4,927	4,802	4,936	6,109	8,301
United States	14,929	20,313	24,567	25,275	24,184	24,795	26,887	26,099	29,410	31,957	42,267
Mexico	358	479	939	1,435	1,520	1,890	2,255	1,884	1,455	1,644	1,591
Guatemala	87	125	71	78	78	56	67	40	58	28	34
Honduras	15	33	36	48	47	45	61	50	101	64	66
El Salvador	65	78	37	40	23	38	42	40	34	29	30
Nicaragua	62	40	16	62	48	73	105	60	42	29	43
Costa Rica	11	11	14	7	11	7	6	7	14	15	19
Panama	88	177	73	132	113	71	166	84	86	71	137
Colombia	94	163	175	151	143	150	152	152	271	226	296

Source: International Monetary Fund. *Direction of Trade Statistics*. Various Editions: 1989, 1988 and 1984. Washington, D.C.

TABLE 6

Japan's Total Energy Requirements, Production, Trade, and Degree of Dependency on Imports (1987)
million metric tons of oil equivalent

		Total Energy Requirements	Indigenous Production, Primary Sources: Total (A)	Crude Oil and NGL[a]	Solid Fuels	Natural Gas	Nuclear Power	Hydro Geothermal, and Solar	Trade: Imports (B)	Exports (C)	Degree of Dependency on Imports $\left(\frac{B-C}{A+B-C}\right)$
Japan	1978	358.33	47.09	0.57	11.18	2.37	14.53	18.44	321.72	1.34	87.2%
	1980	362.10	56.45	0.55	10.90	1.97	20.24	22.78	324.61	3.34	85.1%
	1986	375.06	74.69	0.76	9.37	1.89	41.24	21.43	315.95	5.97	80.6%
	1987	**371.66**	**70.46**	**0.74**	**7.47**	**1.95**	**41.94**	**18.36**	**318.06**	**7.36**	**81.5%**
USA		1,865.7	1,601.37	475.52	563.50	395.66	107.80	58.89	373.73	87.59	15.2%
Germany, F.R.		271.72	129.44	5.49	77.15	13.04	29.15	4.60	162.73	14.99	53.0%
Canada		240.19	289.70	92.40	38.71	70.66	17.26	70.66	38.05	86.03	−19.8%
U.K.		208.67	240.65	126.70	60.15	40.06	12.34	1.39	69.11	102.47	−16.1%
France		206.46	93.21	3.75	10.52	3.34	59.31	16.29	132.18	16.06	55.5%
Italy		148.86	29.02	4.06	1.25	13.50	0.04	10.18	141.63	15.83	81.3%
OECD, total		**3,886.84**	**2,939.57**	**805.57**	**923.95**	**643.44**	**311.85**	**254.76**	**1,636.78**	**619.73**	**25.7%**

a) Natural gas liquid

Sources: OECD. *Energy Balances of OECD Countries.* 1970/1985, 1986/1987.

Yoichi Anzai, Chief Editor. *Japan 1990, An International Comparison.* Tokyo, Japan: Keizai Koho Center (Japan Institute for Social and Economic Affairs), October 1989.

Responding to these economic conditions, plus United States influence to persuade Japan toward liberal trade policies and to stimulate domestic demand, engendered a September 1985 discussion among five major industrialized country finance ministers that led to various policy measures. Economic programs in 1985 and 1986 were attempted to maximize the "utilization of the private sector vitality," but proved more rhetorical due to insufficient funding. As for the "Emergency Economic Measures," implemented by the Japanese government in May 1987, they consisted of public works projects of $34.5 billion and income tax reductions worth $6.9 billion for a total domestic stimulus of $41.4 billion. The Japanese Economic Planning Agency (EPA) estimates the measures increased real GNP in Japanese Fiscal Year (JFY) 1987 by 2 percentage points.

Other structural items considered with policy measures include domestic pricing methods. Amid stronger yen values, vis-à-vis the international market, import prices remained high where they could be utilized to further domestic demand. Factors impeding price adjustments include Japan's distribution system and the oligopolistic structure of numerous Japanese markets. The yen's strong currency value is simply absorbed by the multilayered distribution channels instead of passing on the benefits to the consumer. Coupled with Japan's import restrictions and price controls on agricultural and other products, these barriers are clearly obstacles to favorable price adjustments. Due to these barriers, prices of Japanese food are artificially high in relation to other countries. For example, when compared to United States food prices, Japanese consumer beef prices are three times as expensive and consumer rice prices are four times as expensive. By May 1987, the Economic Council, an advisory panel to the Prime Minister, prepared the Maekawa Report. The Maekawa Report called for economic restructuring and the yen's appreciation was perceived to spur domestic demand, particularly in sectors subject to public regulation, including agriculture, distribution, finance, and petroleum.[18]

Japan - Exchange Arrangements/Exchange Restrictions

International trade items and capital basically flow through Japan freely except for the following administrative controls and restrictions.

Among Japan's prominent exchange arrangements and exchange restrictions, administration of control, imports, payments for invisibles, exports, and capital are considered here as presented in the International Monetary Fund, *Exchange Arrangements and Exchange Restrictions Annual Report 1989*. "The authorities of Japan do not maintain margins in respect of exchange transactions, and exchange rates are determined on the basis of underlying demand and supply conditions in the exchange markets."[19] As for the exchange control system, it is primarily operated by the Ministry of Finance, the Ministry of International Trade and Industry (MITI), and the Bank of Japan as the government's agent. "Import and export reporting requirements are handled by the MITI. Inward direct investments are under the jurisdiction of the Minister of Finance and other appropriate ministers. Outward direct investment requires prior notice to the Minister of Finance."[20]

Except for the seventy-six items included in the Import Restriction System, imports are freely accepted. "For the restricted items, once the importer has obtained authorization from the MITI, he receives an import quota certificate that entitles him to receive an import license from an authorized foreign exchange bank automatically upon application. For the importation of certain other goods from specified areas, individual authorization must be obtained from the MITI."[21] In some instances, payments for imports take as long as two years before the import declaration or after customs clearance. "Longer settlement periods require an import license from the MITI."[22]

The exportable limit for residents and nonresidents is 5 million yen where foreign currency flows are unrestricted. With respect to a resident's overseas deposits with a maturity of less than one year, they are subject to automatic approval by the Bank of Japan for up to 10 million yen. Ranging from export volume, export prices, or other conditions, export restraint may be applied globally or regionally through the jurisdiction of the Export and Import Transaction Law and the Export Trade Control Order issued under the Foreign Exchange and Foreign Trade Control Law. "At the end of 1988, voluntary export restraints and floor prices were applied to exports of certain textile items and machine tools to the United States and the EC, to exports of passenger cars and selected steel products to the United States, and to exports of forklift trucks to the EC. In addition, exports of some other products, including passenger cars to the EC and Sweden and video recorders to the EC were subject to monitoring by the Japanese government."[23] Also, within the jurisdiction of the Foreign Exchange and Foreign Trade Control Law, includes 217 items subject to exportation to socialist countries, or because of a short-supply domestically (as tungsten ore), "or to forestall the imposition of import restrictions by other countries (e.g., on sewing machines and certain textiles)."[24] Individual licenses are required for exports under processing contracts and for exports which payment settlements include an open account or settlement beyond two years. "Exports of specified raw materials for foreign processing and re-import require individual licenses," as well.[25]

In addition to majority equity ownership, or establishment of branch operations, direct investment regulations also encompass:

- "any acquisition of shares in unlisted companies;
- acquisition by a foreign investor of the shares of a listed company (including individual companies for which the stock price in over-the-counter transactions is made public by the Securities Dealers Association) that reaches 10 percent or more when added to those owned by related persons;
- acquisition of loans of more than one-year maturity or securities privately placed in Japan, under certain circumstances."[26]

Direct investment abroad, international loans by residents with repayment terms exceeding two years, and yen-denominated bonds purchased by nonresidents in Japan are subject to prior notice with a 20-day waiting period. International banking by residents and lending in foreign currency "between residents other than those carried out by an authorized bank in Japan require prior approval. Other external transactions by residents may normally be carried out freely."[27]

Japan - Major Investment Trends

Major Japanese investment trends include a burgeoning Tokyo Stock Market, domestic capital improvement activity, direct investment activity abroad and in Japan, and a consortium effort to enter the space industry. Besides strong export earnings, the Tokyo Stock Market generously contributed to Japan's strong cash position during the 1980s. Until recently, numerous economists and other international business analysts believed the undervalued yen served as a major factor in the success of Japanese industry. Today, many analysts believe the major factor in the success of Japanese industry is the inexpensive access to capital at a cost that North American or European companies are unable to acquire. Compared to North American and European stock issues trading in the teens with respect to projected earnings, Japanese price/earnings ratios hover in the forty to fifty-five range. Within this low cost, and high margin scenario, this inexpensive money is easily invested into research and development projects, new technologies, and equipment with a low risk factor.

In addition to inexpensive money, various Japanese stock market shortcomings favor Japanese public firms and the related securities industry with: expensive, fixed commissions on trades; disproportionate dividend payments; and extensive networks of cross-holdings where groups of corporations hold large blocks of shares in other corporations. With cross-holdings, smaller shareholders' opinions are diminished, and hostile takeovers are virtually nonexistent in Tokyo. Until 1987, Japanese equity capital — capital raised from the sale of stock and similar securities — lagged behind the United States equity capital market. In 1986, United States companies raised a record $67.9 billion equity capital, more than double the Japanese level. By 1987, both markets generated approximately $60 billion each. Later in 1987, the United States market dropped substantially where the Tokyo market rebounded swiftly. Attributing to Tokyo's resiliency includes a stronger economy, stronger earnings, stability in the equity market, and strong government regulations. According to Securities Data Company of New York, in the first eight months of 1989, Japanese concerns generated $110 billion compared to $20 billion among American companies.[28] Since the precipitous February 1990 fall in Tokyo's stock market, amid slowing exports and a deteriorating infrastructure, it will prove interesting how Japan will meet its continuing structural challenges.

Even with Japanese direct investment activity increasing 739 percent in the 1978-1988 period since 1951-1977, the Japanese direct investment position ranks among the top five in the world stock of direct investment assets figures. Accounting for Japan's 1988 $47 billion direct investment activity, with a total $186.4 billion in direct overseas investment, Japan's international asset holdings amount to 50 percent of United States direct investments abroad. From 1978 to 1982, direct investment activity increased by 40 percent, from $4.6 billion to $7.7 billion, respectively. From 1983 to 1988, Japanese direct investment activity surged from $8.1 billion to $47 billion, an 83 percent increase (Table 7). One may easily correlate this increased direct investment activity to increasing Japanese import activity since the late 1980s. In essence, the vigorous direct Japanese investments abroad served to shift, or realign, Japan's geographical production base. Favored geographical areas are the United States, the NIEs, and ASEAN.

Numerous Japanese observers believe imports from Japanese subsidiaries abroad have significantly increased with semimanufactured products and finished goods. Even with insufficient data to support this perspective to date, such a close-knit, international network of Japanese suppliers would fit firmly into the Japanese economic philosophy. For such an international supply design is another embodiment of Japanese protectionism superimposed upon the transnational scene vis-à-vis Japanese owned subsidiaries based internationally.

The United States, Panama, the United Kingdom, Indonesia, Hong Kong, Brazil, and the Netherlands rank as the largest recipients of total Japanese direct overseas investments as of March 1989. The United States 39 percentage share of $71.7 billion easily outdistances Panama, the second largest recipient of Japanese direct investment by $59 billion. By March 1988, the United States, the United Kingdom, Switzerland, and Australia received at least 30 percent of their total Japanese direct investment activity; where the Netherlands received 42 percent of their total Japanese investment, 43 percent in Thailand, and 51 percent in Cayman. Favoring North America by 40 percent of total Japanese direct investments abroad, Latin America, Asia, and Europe seem to maintain almost equal representation among Japanese international investors (Table 8). Industries strongly preferred by transnational Japanese investors include finance and insurance, commerce, mining, transportation, and electrical machinery (Table 9).

Foreign direct investment in Japan accounted for $12.8 billion in the 1950-1988 period. United States interests amounted to 49 percent

TABLE 7

Japan's Direct Overseas Investment
(FY 1951- 1988)
Millions of United States Dollars

	Amount [a]
1951 - 1975	15,944
1976	3,462
1977	2,806
1978	4,598
1979	4,995
1980	4,693
1981	8,932
1982	7,703
1983	8,145
1984	10,155
1985	12,217
1986	22,320
1987	33,364
1988	47,022
Total	**186,356**

[a]Figures are the accumulated value of approvals and notification.

Sources: Ministry of Finance, Japan.

Yoichi Anzai, Chief Editor. *Japan 1990, An International Comparison*. Tokyo, Japan: Keizai Koho Center (Japan Institute for Social and Economic Affairs), October 1989.

TABLE 8

Japan's Direct Overseas Investment by Region and Country
As of March 31, 1989
Millions of United States Dollars

	FY 1988 Amount	FY 1951-1988 Total		FY 1988 Amount	FY 1951-1988 Total
U.S.A.	21,701	71,860	Malaysia	387	1,834
Canada	626	3,231	Taiwan	372	1,791
North America, total	**22,328**	**75,091**	Thailand	859	1,992
U.K.	3,956	10,554	Philippines	134	1,120
Luxembourg	657	4,729	**Asia, total**	**5,569**	**32,227**
Netherlands	2,359	5,525	Australia	2,413	8,137
Germany, F.R.	409	2,364	**Oceania, total**	**2,669**	**9,315**
France	463	1,764	Saudi Arabia/Kuwait	20	1,383
Switzerland	454	1,432	**Middle East, total**	**259**	**3,338**
Spain	161	1,045	Panama	1,712	12,858
Europe, total	**9,116**	**30,164**	Brazil	510	5,596
Indonesia	586	9,804	Cayman	2,609	5,085
Hong Kong	1,662	6,167	**South America, total**	**6,428**	**31,617**
Singapore	747	3,812	Liberia	648	3,658
Korea, Rep. of	483	3,248	**Africa, total**	**653**	**4,604**
China	296	2,036	**Total**	**47,022**	**186,356**

[a]Figures are the accumulated value of approvals and notification.

Sources: Ministry of Finance, Japan.

Yoichi Anzai, Chief Editor. *Japan 1990, An International Comparison.* Tokyo, Japan: Keizai Koho Center (Japan Institute for Social and Economic Affairs), October 1989.

TABLE 9

Japan's Direct Overseas Investment by Region and Industry
As of March 31, 1989
Millions of United States Dollars

	North America	Latin America	Asia	Middle East	Europe	Oceania and Africa	Total
Iron & Nonferrous Metals	2,553	1,933	2,268	66	328	522	7,671
Chemicals	2,311	590	1,785	1,128	594	133	6,540
Electrical Machinery	5,952	491	2,414	14	1,261	63	10,196
Transportation Equipment	3,030	1,050	1,183	4	913	776	6,956
Textiles	493	439	1,380	4	303	50	2,669
General Machinery	2,610	378	1,036	11	626	55	4,716
Lumber & Pulp	1,377	200	389	--	5	128	2,099
Manufacturing, total	**23,944**	**5,437**	**12,371**	**1,273**	**4,857**	**1,961**	**49,843**
Mining	1,647	1,557	6,912	393	1,103	2,337	13,949
Commerce	11,693	1,508	1,913	20	3,955	922	20,011
Finance & Insurance	12,370	10,990	2,509	123	14,853	1,031	41,876
Transportation	239	9,235	584	2	101	2,181	12,342
Total	**75,091**	**31,617**	**32,227**	**3,338**	**30,164**	**13,919**	**186,356**
Percentage of Total	40	17	17	2	16	7	

Sources: Ministry of Finance, Japan.

Yoichi Anzai, Chief Editor. ***Japan 1990, An International Comparison.*** Tokyo, Japan: Keizai Koho Center (Japan Institute for Social and Economic Affairs), October 1989.

and Switzerland, the Federal Republic of Germany, and the United Kingdom are ranked a distant second, third, and fourth, respectively, from the United States position. Foreign affiliated companies in Japan comprise $1.65 billion, or 13 percent of foreign direct investment holdings in Japan (Table 10).

As for the Japanese position as a world foreign aid donor, and contributor to multilateral international organizations, Japan's funding levels have substantially expanded since the late 1980s. By 1989, Japan surpassed the United States as the largest annual foreign aid donor. Bilateral aid packages include aid for an $850 million set of loans for the Mexican smog challenge, to a $5 billion soft loan package to China for modernization projects; this Chinese project is Japan's largest assistance project to date. Within the multinational organizational realm, Japan's new International Monetary Fund (IMF) second position — shared with West Germany — was ascertained after the United States agreed to a 50 percent increase in the IMF's capital resources, or quotas, in return for a tougher policy toward delinquent members. "Providing the quota is increased by 1991, the Fund's resources will increase from $120 billion to $180 billion."[29] Japan and West Germany will share an equal second position behind the United States, and Britain and France are equal partners for the number three slot. "There has been great resistance to Japan's bid for second place, which Tokyo has long argued was justified in view of its growing financial power and aid contributions to the developing world."[30]

Since the space shuttle Challenger disaster in January 1986, the international private sector space industry expanded. The Japanese entrance into the industry proved sluggish due to their H-1's vehicle ineffective power to launch large satellites. Countering this inefficiency, a consortium of Japanese companies, led by Mitsubishi Heavy Industries, is developing the H-2. Scheduled launch date is early 1993, a year behind schedule due to the rocket's liquid fuel engine design. The H-2 will be Japan's first commercial enterprise to launch private satellites. At $100 million per launch, Japan's launch expenses surpass the competition: Europe's Arianspace, NASA, including the Chinese and Russian space programs.

Among the consortium, various companies are responsible for the H-2 design: NEC, Toshiba, Nissan, Hitachi, Fujitsu, Kawasaki Heavy Industries, Ishikawajima-Harima Heavy Industries, Mitsubishi Electric

TABLE 10

Foreign Direct Investment in Japan by Country
As of March 31, 1989
Millions of United States Dollars

	FY 1988 Amount	FY 1950-1988 Total
U.S.A.	1,701	6,268
Switzerland	273	928
Germany F.R.	195	546
U.K.	112	518
Netherlands	157	482
Hong Kong	44	390
France	27	202
Canada	22	152
Foreign Affiliated Companies in Japan	306	1,653
Other	332	1,655
Total	**3,243**	**12,794**

Sources: Ministry of Finance, Japan

Yoichi Anzai, Chief Editor. *Japan 1990, An International Comparison*. Tokyo, Japan: Keizai Koho Center (Japan Institute for Social and Economic Affairs), October 1989.

and Mitsubishi Heavy Industries. Approximately seventy-seven companies will participate in the space program. In perspective of size comparisons, the H-2 is compatible to a mid-size automobile where the H-1 is similar to an economy car. Within rocket comparisons, the H-2 is substantially smaller than the most powerful United States rockets, the Titan 3 and Titan 4. The H-2 capabilities could place a two-ton satellite into stationary orbit, or launch a ten-ton satellite in low Earth orbit. The Japanese government will fund H-2 development. Testing the H-2 will be under the operational administration of the National Space Development Agency of Japan (NASDA). By July 1990, a new company will be formed to purchase the H-2 from Mitsubishi Heavy Industries. Usually programs in other countries are subsidized and/or developed by the military. "Because of a ban on producing offensive weapons imposed after World War Two, Japan's military has no rockets, so the cost of the rocket is borne by the civilian space agency".[31]

Since the middle 1980s, Japan's major investment trends have strongly reflected record export-earnings and strong equity capital fund raising. Subsequently, direct investment abroad, foreign aid, and contributions to the multinational fora have grown substantially. Awash with cash and expanding international recognition, Japan is plagued with basic structural challenges. These challenges range from an ailing transportation infrastructure, inadequate health services for an aging population, and numerous economic impediments from ineffective consumer price adjustment mechanisms to strong import protection schemes. Coupled with a foreign dependence for integral natural resources, Japan's new economic capabilities and economic resources are more vulnerable than many individuals believe.

Australia - The Economic Context and Trade Policy

Located in the Southwest Quarter of the Pacific Rim Region, Australia is an advanced, medium-sized economy, ranking tenth among OECD members in terms of GDP. Since the middle 1940s, Australia's population virtually doubled through an elaborate, planned immigration program. Approximately 4.5 million migrants settled in Australia from 1945 through 1987, where about 80 percent have remained. To date, one in five Australians are foreign born. The largest postwar immigrants were from Britain and Ireland, followed by Italy, Greece, and Yugoslavia. Since the 1960s, immigrants from Latin America, the Middle East, and Asia comprised the primary immigrant sources. Since 1975, Australia has accepted more than 114,000 Indochinese from Cambodia, Laos, and Vietnam. On a per capita basis, Australia has more Indochinese refugees as permanent residents than any other country.

Australia is considered a relatively open market with an export base comprised of agricultural and mineral commodities, and imports are primarily manufactures of industrial supplies and capital goods. Exports consist of 20 percent of Australia's GDP. For some products in Australia's agricultural and mineral sectors, 75 percent or more of output is sold internationally. Australia is the world's largest exporter of wool, alumina, coal, refined lead and mineral sands, and a major exporter of bauxite, iron ore, beef, veal, sheep, aluminum, gold and zinc. Both agricultural and mining sectors are efficient, internationally competitive, and account for about 40 percent of Australia's merchandise exports. Due to Australia's position as a major exporter of minerals, agricultural produce, and other commodities, the Australian Dollar is the sixth most traded international currency. Although a resource-rich country, services account for two-thirds of GDP. Until recently, numerous service industries were strongly regulated, including financial intermediaries. Throughout its history, Australia has sustained its capital importer position on both private and public accounts, reflecting an average current account deficit of about 2.5 percent of GDP during the previous two decades. Japan, the United States, the United Kingdom, South Korea, and Hong Kong constitute Australia's major export partners. As for import markets, Australia's primary suppliers include Japan, West Germany, the United States, the United Kingdom, Taiwan, and New Zealand. Leading Pacific Rim Region export markets, within the billion dollar category, range from Japan, the United States, Hong Kong, New Zealand, South Korea, Taiwan, and Singapore. Except for Canada, the United States, and Mexico, Australia's Northeast Quarter and Southeast Quarter export activity remains weak. In 1988, on the import side, most frequent suppliers include the United States, Japan, New Zealand, and Taiwan (Table 11).

TABLE 11

Australia's Bilateral Trade with Pacific Rim Region, Selected Members
1978-1988
Millions of United States Dollars

Exports

	1978	1979	1980	1981	1982	1983	1984	1985	1986	1987	1988
Northwest Quarter											
Japan	4,382	5,197	5,871	6,136	5,703	5,697	6,150	6,295	6,065	6,791	8,881
Soviet Union	301	563	1,137	712	693	483	594	594	698	487	561
North Korea	9	21	41	6	4	11	22	22	28	36	43
South Korea	408	501	486	769	709	788	862	862	928	1,079	1,545
China, People's Republic	484	776	796	639	838	393	736	865	1,065	1,071	866
Taiwan	322	454	512	593	643	581	645	701	744	885	1,141
Hong Kong	296	354	330	431	425	379	698	572	511	975	1,649
Philippines	151	183	192	189	177	156	98	137	119	199	252
Laos	....	....	1	....	....	....	....	....	....	....	....
Vietnam	9	23	43	9	1	2	2	2	5	4	10
Kampuchea	....	....	7	....	....	....	....	....	....	....	....
Thailand	104	135	159	156	155	194	178	122	129	182	299
Myanmar	5	9	13	10	10	4	4	3	5	5	3
Malaysia	343	394	507	518	431	476	468	388	368	424	538
Singapore	274	377	538	533	722	651	816	619	441	642	1,038
Brunei	2	4	3	4	5	7	8	7	7	10	11
Southwest Quarter											
Indonesia	236	280	370	469	399	363	310	322	373	367	480
Papua New Guinea	293	378	474	470	481	467	462	379	392	509	615
New Zealand	720	922	1,043	1,110	1,130	1,120	1,406	1,062	1,031	1,511	1,630
Solomon Islands	13	18	28	24	20	36	30	29	27	28	56
Fiji	101	148	168	203	175	162	154	144	117	93	117
New Caledonia	26	43	44	48	46	34	34	26	30	49	67
Tonga	3	5	6	7	9	6	5	5	6	11	11

TABLE 11 (continued)

Australia's Bilateral Trade with Pacific Rim Region, Selected Members 1978-1988 Millions of United States Dollars

Exports

	1978	1979	1980	1981	1982	1983	1984	1985	1986	1987	1988
Southwest Quarter (continued)											
Tuvalu	....	....	....	1	2	1	1	1	1	2	1
Vanuatu	22	16	16	14	13	14	16	13	13	17	21
Nauru	10	13	21	17	10	12	7	10	10	10	10
Kiribati	9	10	12	8	7	10	7	5	9	8	9
Southeast Quarter											
Ecuador	9	5	6	12	6	3	13	9	2	2	6
Peru	7	6	12	11	9	3	7	11	13	18	26
Chile	2	16	19	9	3	7	8	8	11	15	18
Western Samoa	6	8	10	6	6	7	6	10	9	8	21
French Polynesia	9	12	12	14	13	16	12	20	37	54	56
Northeast Quarter											
Canada	287	352	470	428	347	298	262	251	372	436	606
United States	1,632	2,220	2,570	2,438	2,248	2,115	2,646	2,344	2,389	3,001	3,508
Mexico	24	28	234	42	20	9	40	63	24	30	48
Guatemala	3	3	1	4	1	....	....	....	....	....	....
Honduras	....	....	....	....	....	....	....	....	....	....	....
El Salvador	3	4	....	1	....	....	....	....	....	....	....
Nicaragua	2	....	....	....	....	....	....	....	....	3	....
Costa Rica	1	....	1	....	....	....	....	....	....	....	....
Panama	2	10	2	2	9	1	2	2	1	....	....
Colombia	....	....	....	....	....	2	1	11	16	5	9

TABLE 11 (continued)

Australia's Bilateral Trade with Pacific Rim Region, Selected Members
1978-1988
Millions of United States Dollars

Imports

	1978	1979	1980	1981	1982	1983	1984	1985	1986	1987	1988
Northwest Quarter											
Japan	2,711	2,580	3,477	4,688	4,865	4,264	5,115	5,430	5,348	5,321	6,713
Soviet Union	73	65	18	10	13	10	24	8	8	12	29
North Korea	....	....	....	....	....	....	....	....	1	....	....
South Korea	....	....	....	....	....	278	384	357	463	696	8687
China, People's Republic	140	166	244	340	319	230	313	292	333	480	695
Taiwan	333	419	539	676	643	634	854	792	882	1,202	1,400
Hong Kong	347	388	452	518	534	433	532	477	493	586	676
Philippines	73	92	94	109	91	75	87	86	78	85	106
Laos	....	....	....	....	....	....	....	1	....	....	....
Vietnam	1	....	....	....	....	4	4	7	8	13	17
Kampuchea	....	1	....	....	....	....	....	....	....	....	....
Thailand	37	48	69	81	78	93	122	126	160	221	281
Myanmar	1	1	6	....	1	1	3	1	1	1	1
Malaysia	149	200	219	212	203	168	251	237	255	328	483
Singapore	274	360	605	647	720	414	539	578	480	560	759
Brunei	....	....	....	30	....	15	....	....	12	24	13
Southwest Quarter											
Indonesia	121	211	397	470	741	229	340	179	190	366	317
Papua New Guinea	77	81	96	85	63	67	77	96	129	107	80
New Zealand	438	545	692	776	730	685	876	956	918	1,110	1,463
Solomon Islands	....	1	1	1	1	1	1	1	2	1	2
Fiji	11	17	21	19	25	24	32	31	31	28	51
New Caledonia	....	....	1	3	1	1	2	2	2	2	2
Tonga	....	2	3	2	2	1	2	2	2	2	2
Tuvalu	....	....	....	....	....	....	....	....	....	....	....

TABLE 11 (continued)

Australia's Bilateral Trade with Pacific Rim Region, Selected Members 1978-1988 Millions of United States Dollars

Imports

	1978	1979	1980	1981	1982	1983	1984	1985	1986	1987	1988
Southwest Quarter (continued)											
Vanuatu	....	....	....	....	....	....	....	....	1	....	1
Nauru	50	57	79	71	56	70	48	40	46	48	62
Kiribati	13	9	1	....	....	....	....	....	....	....	....
Southeast Quarter											
Ecuador	1	1	2	3	3	4	4	3	4	4	4
Peru	1	1	2	3	3	3	7	3	2	4	7
Chile	1	1	6	6	2	2	4	6	7	17	22
Western Samoa	1	1	1	....	1	2	2	3	2	2	3
French Polynesia	4	3	2	4	3	2	9	10	11	17	27
Northeast Quarter											
Canada	338	485	556	618	546	378	466	470	476	551	757
United States	3,146	3,774	4,434	5,477	5,264	4,265	5,132	5,249	5,235	5,784	7,228
Mexico	9	17	20	25	28	27	33	44	39	39	53
Guatemala	....	1	1	1	1	1	....	2	....	....	1
Honduras	....	....	....	....	....	....	....	....	....	....	....
El Salvador	....	....	....	....	....	....	....	....	....	....	....
Nicaragua	....	....	....	1	1	....	1	....	....	....	....
Costa Rica	1	1	1	1	1	1	1	2	1	1	1
Panama	....	2	....	....	....	....	....	....	....	....	....
Colombia	....	....	....	....	....	6	2	2	3	4	5

Source: International Monetary Fund. *Direction of Trade Statistics*. Various Editions: 1989, 1988 and 1984. Washington, D.C.

Similar to Japan's vulnerability to world commodity prices, Australia's sensitivities to world commodity price fluctuations are experienced from a supplier's perspective rather than from an importer's position like that of Japan. For example, in the early 1970s, developing countries earning substantial oil revenues precipitated a dramatic expansion in agricultural imports. By the early 1980s, this income was redistributed among developed nations, thus contracting agricultural imports among oil suppliers in developing countries. Commodity source countries, as Australia, experienced the international recession of the early 1980s, coupled with low commodity price levels between 1984 and 1987. Exacerbating this situation were high import tariffs and direct government assistance programs aiding numerous Australian industries, which created distortions and impediments to economic growth. Although substantial domestic assistance is still intact in textile, clothing and footwear, passenger motor vehicles, along with dairy and tobacco industries, direct assistance programs and tariffs are shrinking. By 1992, ongoing import tariff reductions are slated for an average 5.5 percent drop from 1986-87 levels. Since mid-1987, commodity prices have risen markedly, as strong growth in world economic activity continued during commodity supply restraints. Fiber and metal markets expanded in 1987. By 1988, consumption was more broadly based among dairy, sugar, and cereal prices. With increased demand and a constrained commodity supply, aided by the 1987 North American drought, cereal prices appreciated further.

Amid stronger commodity prices and economic restructuring, in terms of industry and trade policies, the Australian economy began overheating in mid-1988. With a sustained appreciation of the currency, inflation at 7.6 percent (the highest inflation rate among OECD members), imports surged and the current account deficit expanded. In order to provide a "soft landing" for the economy, the government maintained a firm fiscal policy and tightened monetary policy. In Austrailian Fiscal Year (AFY) 1988/89, the federal government experienced its first balanced budget in 35 years, and by July 1989 the prime interest rate reached 20.25 percent. In AFY 1989/90, the current $4.4 billion budget surplus will either be equalled or surpassed. By July 1990, the Australian prime interest rate moved to 18 percent, where chronic current account deficits, an expanding external debt, a low savings level, high unemployment, and continued vulnerability to world commodity price fluctuations exemplified the Australian market throughout the 1980s.

Dependent on exports for 30 percent of its GDP, Australia's primary commodities accounted for some 75 percent of merchandise exports in 1988-89. Within this atmosphere, Australia is most vulnerable to world commodity price fluctuations and discriminatory trade practices among its trading partners. In an effort to enhance export activity and beneficial trade relations, Australia actively maintains numerous bilateral trade agreements with many of its major trading partners, participates in a variety of trade-oriented multilateral organizations, and maintains representation in all major markets. Bilateral agreements usually include reciprocal favored nation treatment for imports, close consultation on trade matters, and the operation of a joint committee or commission. Bilateral trade agreements also may entail industrial and technical cooperation as well as business investment opportunities. Among regional multilateral organizational affiliations include the ASEAN/Australia Economic Co-operation Program (AAECP), and the South Pacific Regional Trade and Economic Co-operation Agreement (SPARTECA). AAECP, established in 1974, currently contributes significantly to intra-ASEAN cooperation, according to the AAECP 1986-87 review process. Based on this review, a second phase of AAECP began in July 1989 emphasizing stronger ASEAN-Australia relations. AAECP Phase II focuses on two project areas: 1) science and technology, and 2) food and agriculture. With time, the primary focus will favor science and technology along with trade and investment promotion.[32] SPARTECA provides unrestricted, duty-free access to Australia and New Zealand for South Pacific Forum Island members. SPARTECA terms and conditions are discussed on page 72 in the following Exchange Arrangements and Exchange Restrictions section.

As for specific Australian trade policy objectives, they include five primary points:

- "maintaining an open international trade and payments system;

- maintaining an equitable framework of multilateral rules based on non-discrimination, predictability and transparency which provides for progressive trade liberalization;

- ensuring fair and reasonable access to markets for agricultural products, restraints on subsidized competition in third world markets and stability in commodity markets;

- achieving fair and stable prices for minerals and market security; and

- promoting employment through increased exports in general and increased exports of manufactures and services in particular."[33]

The GATT observes the main features of the Australian import system as: "the dominance of the tariff; relatively little use of non-tariff measures; an ongoing program to reduce border protection; and regular assessment and reform of measures which enhance transparency, and to reduce the extent of administrative discretion in the application of measures."[34] Due to the May 1988 Economic Statement, by 1992, the average import tariff will decline by one-third, to 5.5 percent from its 1986-87 level. GATT continues with the main features of Australia's export system: "The majority of Australia's exports receive no direct assistance; direct assistance to exports is modest, falling and most is subject to scrutiny in the budget; and export of Australian commodities is relatively unrestricted."[35] Quality control, conservation, defense, other national interests, and international agreement obligations justify Australian export controls. Provided on a cost-sharing basis with industry, export inspections are administered by the government.

Australia - Exchange Arrangements/Exchange Restrictions

In compliance with International Monetary Fund reporting requirements, Australia's distinctive exchange arrangements and exchange restrictions, as of 31 December 1988, include administration of control, imports, exports, and capital. The Australian Dollar is

Australia's currency and circulates in numerous countries including Kiribati, Nauru, and Tuvalu. Exchange rates are determined by demand and supply forces within the exchange market where "the Reserve Bank sets a limit for each dealer's net open overnight foreign exchange exposure."[36] As for foreign currency futures contracts and options on futures, they are traded on the Sydney Futures Exchange. Payments in foreign exchange or other means of payment must be accompanied with a taxation clearance certificate issued by the Australian Taxation Office when presented to authorized foreign exchange dealers. Specifically covered under the taxation clearance provision are "certain transactions with residents of designated countries and areas, and for emigrants' remittances in excess of A$50,000 or its foreign currency equivalent to all countries."[37] Designated countries and areas consist of the Bahamas, Bermuda, British Channel Islands, British Virgin Islands, Cayman Islands, Gibraltar, Grenada, Hong Kong, Isle of Man, Liberia, Liechtenstein, Luxembourg, Nauru, the Netherlands Antillies, Switzerland, Tonga, and Vanuatu. Within undesignated countries and areas, outflows exceeding A$50,000 or its foreign currency equivalent, are required to be declared through the auspices of foreign exchange dealers with respect to monetary values in terms of investments, gifts, sustenance and trust distributions, loans or loan repayments, travel expenditure, remittances connected with futures operations overseas and payments of interest, dividends, service fees, or royalties.[38]

Imports and import payments are primarily unrestricted in Australia. Licensing requirements prevail for an assortment of second-hand equipment, which includes ships and aircraft. What tariff quotas do exist — for most textiles, clothing, and footwear — are imposed with respect to health, community protection, or to sustain quality standards. By 1995, these tariff quotas are planned to be eliminated through "out-of-quota" tariff rates. According to the May 1988 Economic Statement, certain agricultural products and manufactured imports tariffs are slated for tariff rate reductions. Through annual reductions, rates exceeding 15 percent are to be reduced to 15 percent, where 15 percent tariff rates and lower will be reduced to 10 percent. By 1992, passenger motor vehicle tariff reductions will reach 35 percent. Excluded from the phased tariff reduction program of May 1988 consists of passenger motor vehicles, textiles, clothing and footwear, and the shipbuilding industry is assisted by production subsidies. Lowered to 15 percent, chemicals and plastics tariffs will remain unchanged.

Other import arrangements described by the International Monetary Fund, *Exchange Arrangements and Exchange Restrictions Annual Report 1989*, entail the Australia-New Zealand Closer Economic Relations Trade Agreement (ANZCERTA), and the South Pacific Regional Trade and Economic Co-operation Agreement (SPARTECA). ANZCERTA provided for free trade in goods by 1 July 1990 with New Zealand. Imported New Zealand motor vehicles were subject to import duties till January 1990. Textiles and footwear quotas were abolished by March 1989 and New Zealand liquid milk and cheese were fully liberalized in July 1990. In the event of below-market, New Zealand product price competition, Australian domestic legislative measures replaced antidumping actions by July 1990. Exclusions of the ANZCERTA agreement encompass telecommunications, postal services, media, banking, airport services, and aviation. Within the South Pacific Forum membership, SPARTECA allows unrestricted, duty-free access to Australian and New Zealand markets for most products originating from island members. Members of the South Pacific Forum include New Zealand, Australia, the Cook Island, Fiji, Kiribati, Nauru, Niue, Papua New Guinea, the Solomon Islands, Tonga, Tuvalu, Vanuatu, and Western Samoa.

As for exports, permits or licenses are only required with respect to items designated by the Export Control Act, Customs (Prohibited Exports) Regulations, Protection of Moveable Cultural Heritage Act, and the Wildlife Protection Regulation of Exports and Imports Act. Exports of specified minerals, metals, hydrocarbons, and nuclear-sensitive material is prohibited in accordance to the Customs (Prohibited Exports) Regulations unless approved by the Minister for Primary Industries and Energy or by the Department of Primary Industries and Energy to export alumina, bauxite, coal, iron ore, uranium, and other nuclear-oriented materials. With respect to uranium sales, contracts must meet Ministerial Determinations requirements as provided by the three uranium producers. In order to export monazite and xenotime, nuclear materials, approval under the requirements of the government's nuclear safeguards policy must be met. In contrast, automatic export approvals are extended to applications with specified time periods with respect to the following: ores, concentrates, nitrates, matte and oxides of copper, lead, manganese, nickel (except nickel powder) and zinc, blister and refined copper, lead bullion, salt, petroleum products, and liquefied petroleum gas and condensate. Quotas apply to secondary copper ingots and other basic shapes made from scrap metal, and exports of copper scrap and copper alloy scrap are embargoed.

From the standpoint of capital arrangements, direct investment by nonresidents in Australia is "based on the recognition that foreign investment makes a substantial contribution to the development of Australia's industries and resources."[39] Knowledge of foreign ownership and foreign control of Australian industries and resources is paramount to Australia's foreign investment policy. Within the parameters of the Foreign Takeovers Act 1975, the Foreign Investment Review Board examines investment proposals by international business interests. Types of investment proposals constitute: "those involving the establishment of a new business or project, irrespective of size, in the media and civil aviation sectors, or in other sectors where the total amount of the investment is A$10 million or more (including diversification into activities not previously undertaken directly in Australia and new projects in mining and primary industries); those involving direct investment by foreign governments or their agencies (excluding investments related to their official representation); and proposals to acquire real estate and undertake real estate development projects."[40]

The Foreign Takeover Act 1975 also covers foreign interest acquisition of companies or businesses operating in Australia. Proposals or alterations of nonresident's status among nonresident-controlled corporations or businesses must notify the government with respect to the nonresident's substantial interest in a company. A substantial foreign interest is defined as any interest of "15 percent or more in the ownership or voting power of a corporation or business by a single foreign interest, either alone or together with associates, or an interest of 40 percent or more in aggregate in the ownership or voting power of a corporation or business by two or more foreign interests and their associates."[41] Civil aviation and media sector investment proposals are considered case-by-case, where acquisitions of existing non-oil and gas mining projects over A$5 million are approved providing adequate economic benefits are demonstrated.[42] Serving as an independent, government intermediary, the Foreign Investment Review Board advises the government on foreign investment activities, and assists international investors with investment proposals.

For those foreign investors inclined to increase Australian participation in their operation, such a "naturalization" process provides an economic incentive. With increased Australian participation, foreign-owned operations are offered equity-oriented credit which facilitates majority Australian ownership for mining projects and related ventures.

Australia - Major Investment Trends

Australia's investment trends include export promotion activities, an urban residential real estate boom, surging private sector debt levels, and expanding direct investment activity in Australia and abroad. Designed to promote export activity, the Australian Trade Commission (AUSTRADE) was established in 1985. AUSTRADE export services range from counseling, planning, to developing export strategies along with support and promotional activities. AUSTRADE's financial support and services include:

- The Export Market Development Scheme;
- The Innovative Agricultural Marketing Program;
- The High Technology Exporters Scheme; and
- The International Business Development Scheme.

The Export Market Development Scheme, for example, reimburses marketing expenses, in part, as travel and promotional costs to assist Australian firms. This scheme is designed to assist small companies with the financial burdens associated with up-front planning and marketing costs. Reimbursements only occur after the cost is incurred, and is classified as a claim providing the:

- "maximum export income ceiling is A$20 million per corporation;
- grants are determined on the basis of 70 percent of eligible expenditure in excess of A$10,000;
- the maximum grant is A$200,000 but after two grants the maximum is the lesser of A$200,000 or a certain percentage of export earnings;
- the maximum is reduced to A$150,000 for the ninth grant and to $A 100,000 for the tenth and subsequent grants; and
- minimum export expenditure threshold is A$10,000."[43]

Other financial support and services provided by AUSTRADE concerns the Export Finance and Insurance Corporation (EFIC) activities. EFIC services consist of export finance, finance guarantees and indemnities, export credit insurance, and overseas investment insurance. As an incentive, AUSTRADE services are provided free of charge for two years. In 1988-89, export financial assistance amounted to $238 million, a decline in real terms of almost 4 percent from 1987-1988.[44]

In terms of domestic performance, since the 1987 stock market crash, investors moved from equities into urban real estate properties. Embodied within an expanding economic climate fueled with higher commodity prices and deregulation within the financial markets, interest rates rose in an effort to stem inflationary pressures. By the early 1980s, international debt accounted for A$7.1 billion or 5.8 percent of GDP. At the end of 1989, private foreign debt totalled A$108 billion, or 32.2 percent of GDP, extraordinarily high by any indices. Since the public sector currently maintains balanced accounts, Australia's external debt situation is unique since it entails private sector borrowings. With increasing foreign debt activity in Australia, business investment spending at an annual rate of 15.5 percent in 1988-1989 was stronger than the 15 percent increase in 1987-1988. As one would surmise, the Australian government would anticipate this as a contributing factor to productive capital investments, to increase Australian production capacity and reduce its reliance on imports.

With private investments in housing at a real rate of 24.4 percent during 1987-1988, compared to the 11.5 percent rise in 1986-1987, the domestic housing market registered as one of the strongest sectors. Coupled with other areas of consumer spending, as increasing merchandise import levels, these economic indicators tend to counter any substantial capital investment activity spurred by international borrowings.

Throughout the 1982-83 to 1987-88 period, total foreign investment activity in Australia averaged an annual increase of A$24 billion. Responding to Australia's economic upturn with stronger international commodity prices, direct investment activity increased A$29.4 billion in 1984 and A$36.37 billion in 1986. On a bilateral basis, the United Kingdom is the ranking foreign investor in Australia followed by the United States and Japan as of 1987-88. From a multilateral perspective, ASEAN accounts for 5.7 percent of the OECD's foreign investment activity in Australia during 1987-88. The OECD's investment activity continues to expand consecutively through the 1982-87 period, where ASEAN's investment commitments subsided in 1985 and 1987 (Table 12).

Proposed by Japanese interests in 1987, Australia is a probable site for a $9.75 billion "city of the future." This new urban center would incorporate industries, research, training, education, and leisure for the 21st century. As a *multifunction polis*, this urban center could support approximately 250,000 skilled workers from North America, Europe, Asia, Australia, and New Zealand. Approximately 103 Japanese companies were persuaded by the Japanese government to participate in this project. On the Japanese side, EIE International is a key property management group involved with the project, where Anderson Consulting and Kinhill Engineers are providing Australian management options for the project. Though strong Australian public opposition persisted, it remains to be seen how this venture will proceed.[45]

Australian investment abroad steadily expanded in 1982-83 to 1987-88 by 68 percent. The United States, the United Kingdom, and New Zealand are major recipients of Australian investment abroad. The United Kingdom figures indicate a strong growing commitment from 1985 through 1987, while in smaller dollar figures, the New Zealand foreign investment commitment has been steadily increasing

TABLE 12

Foreign Investment in Australia, by Country, 1982-1988
Millions of Australian Dollars

Country of Investor	1982-83	1983-84	1984-85	1985-86	1986-87	1987-88
LEVELS OF FOREIGN INVESTMENT						
OECD--						
USA	17,632	20,320	26,819	31,903	40,845	39,234
Japan	9,277	10,802	16,200	20,840	21,321	26,515
Switzerland	3,119	3,114	4,050	5,856	7,502	7,439
EEC--						
UK	18,781	20,631	26,138	29,318	37,127	44,019
Other (a)	7,409	8,054	10,441	14,443	17,842	18,461
Total	26,190	28,685	36,579	43,761	54,968	62,479
Other OECD (a)	2,010	2,844	3,801	4,541	8,888	8,200
Total OECD	58,228	65,764	87,449	106,901	133,523	143,867
ASEAN (b)	4,898	7,214	9,695	8,951	10,477	8,175
Other Countries (b)	4,415	5,062	6,840	5,803	6,862	7,737
International Capital Markets	985	1,425	4,466	13,306	20,801	25,428
International Institutions	533	390	341	365	332	239
Unallocated	1,876	2,017	2,527	4,111	3,808	5,534
Total	**70,935**	**81,873**	**111,318**	**139,437**	**175,803**	**190,980**
CAPITAL TRANSACTIONS						
OECD--						
USA	498	1,411	3,564	4,304	4,469	433
Japan	3,217	1,500	3,454	2,673	761	5,256
Switzerland	208	134	399	544	334	650
EEC--						
UK	2,419	2,529	2,287	1,932	3,561	6,721
Other (a)	1,004	656	1,290	3,051	1,768	725
Total	3,423	3,185	3,577	4,983	5,330	7,446
Other OECD (a)	147	242	402	871	1,821	1,371
Total OECD	7,493	6,473	11,397	13,374	12,713	15,157
ASEAN (b)	1,619	2,148	592	-837	1,003	69
Other Countries (b)	1,230	586	71	-760	1,168	1,676
International Capital Markets	161	953	2,321	6,806	6,791	5,125
International Institutions	86	-137	-55	14	-24	-94
Unallocated	-140	145	462	548	-354	1,034
Total	**10,449**	**10,167**	**14,788**	**19,144**	**21,298**	**22,967**

TABLE 12 (continued)

Foreign Investment in Australia, by Country, 1982-1988
Millions of Australian Dollars

Country of Investor	1982-83	1983-84	1984-85	1985-86	1986-87	1987-88
	INVESTMENT INCOME					
OECD--						
USA	828	1,707	2,037	2,486	3,077	3,755
Japan	478	799	1,224	1,646	1,805	1,851
Switzerland	150	175	213	275	401	403
EEC--						
UK	1,012	1,504	1,833	2,049	2,301	2,405
Other (a)	265	452	524	784	1,152	1,447
Total	1,277	1,956	2,357	2,833	3,453	3,853
Other OECD (a)	100	192	212	327	321	371
Total OECD	2,834	4,829	6,041	7,567	9,057	10,233
ASEAN (b)	288	470	739	694	613	481
Other Countries (b)	244	327	440	393	336	336
International Capital Markets	5	38	124	555	934	1,516
International Institutions	55	40	32	24	22	
22						
Unallocated	116	130	187	256	381	936
Total	**3,542**	**5,833**	**7,563**	**9,489**	**11,343**	**13,525**

(a) Until 1985-86, Spain and Portugal are included in "Other OECD," from 1985-86 they are included in "Other EEC."

(b) Until 1983-84, Brunei is included in "Other Countries," from 1983-84 it is included in "ASEAN."

Source: Castles, Ian. *Yearbook Australia 1989*. Number 72. Canberra: Australian Bureau of Statistics, 1989.

as well, from A$927 million to A$4.96 billion, in 1984 and 1987, respectively (Table 13). Another aspect of Australian foreign investment concerns Australia's Foreign Aid Program. "The objective of the Australian Aid program is to promote the economic and social advancement of the peoples of developing countries in response to Australia's humanitarian concerns. It also promotes Australia's foreign policy and commercial interests...contributing to growth with equity as a key challenge facing Australia in delivering an effective aid program."[46] Leading recipients of Australian Aid flows include Papua New Guinea, Indonesia, and Malaysia where Indo-China Regional, Vietnam, and Laos rounded out the list in 1987-88. (Table 14)

Chile - The Economic Context and Trade Policy

Located 7,064 miles east of Australia from Sydney to Santiago, Chile flanks the majority of western South America. Situated west of Argentina and Bolivia, and south of Peru, Chile's economic performance is recovering strongly from a mismanaged external debt burden and a 1982 14 percent GDP decline: six consecutive years of economic growth since 1983; the gross domestic product expanded by 7.3 percent where per capita GDP almost exceeded the 1981 historical high; inflation and unemployment declined substantially; savings, investments, and real income increased; and external accounts and public sector finances continued to approach more favorable levels. Given Chile's depressed condition in 1982, such a set of economic indicators for any consecutive seven-year period is impressive. Spanning 2,650 miles along the Pacific coast, Chile's urban population and commercial activity are concentrated in the central zone, which includes Santiago, the capital, and Valparaiso. Compared to the central zone's Mediterranean climate, northern desert mining activities in natural nitrate, elemental iodine, and metallic lithium are located within the moderate climatic effects of the Pacific Ocean's Humboldt Current and the Andes Mountains. In the north, the Atacama Desert is home to an estimated 21 to 33 percent of the world's known metallic lithium reserves and the world's largest nitrate deposits. Replete with winding waterways, islands, fjords, to forests, volcanoes, lakes, and grazing lands, southern Chile's marine climate offers continuous geographic challenges

TABLE 13

Australian Investment Abroad, by Country, 1982-1988
Millions of Australian Dollars

Country of Investor	1982-83	1983-84	1984-85	1985-86	1986-87	1987-88
LEVELS OF AUSTRALIAN INVESTMENT						
OECD--						
USA	8,106	10,195	11,906	13,081	20,880	19,303
New Zealand	781	928	927	1,599	3,785	4,957
UK	883	1,465	2,511	3,652	7,531	12,288
Other OECD (a)	3,019	3,939	6,399	9,848	12,656	14,118
Total OECD	12,789	16,528	21,744	28,180	44,852	50,665
ASEAN (b)	1,877	1,676	1,582	1,357	1,413	1,079
Papua New Guinea	850	1,016	994	856	1,437	1,803
Other Countries (b)	2,478	3,059	3,977	7,038	7,222	9,262
Reserve Bank Gold (c)	3,744	3,478	3,772	4,014	4,951	4,509
Unallocated	780	949	1,691	1,838	1,555	2,549
Total	**22,518**	**26,706**	**33,760**	**43,283**	**61,430**	**69,868**
CAPITAL TRANSACTIONS						
OECD--						
USA	2,228	2,186	-307	1,294	7,626	1,648
New Zealand	148	163	231	2	1,604	1,061
UK	1	225	717	788	1,142	4,731
Other OECD (a)	1,264	968	1,521	1,000	1,402	2,142
Total OECD	3,640	3,543	2,161	3,084	11,774	9,582
ASEAN (a)	157	285	319	111	75	2
Papua New Guinea	149	230	94	-107	13	n.p.
Other Countries (b)	299	231	351	2,230	594	2,560
Unallocated	-123	157	231	-456	-81	n.p.
Total	**4,122**	**4,446**	**3,156**	**4,862**	**12,375**	**14,393**

TABLE 13 (continued)

Australian Investment Abroad, by Country, 1982-1988
Millions of Australian Dollars

Country of Investor	1982-83	1983-84	1984-85	1985-86	1986-87	1987-88
	INVESTMENT INCOME					
OECD--						
USA	468	643	698	405	517	654
New Zealand	101	154	173	262	344	47
UK	107	122	96	277	330	672
Other OECD (a)	82	119	270	396	437	634
Total OECD	758	1,037	1,237	1,340	1,628	2,007
ASEAN (b)	93	150	101	154	121	82
Papua New Guinea	47	108	53	141	61	3
Other Countries (b)	103	118	80	212	600	1,043
Unallocated	53	55	54	118	219	70
Total	**1,054**	**1,468**	**1,525**	**1,966**	**2,628**	**3,205**

(a) The foreign exchange part of reserve assets, with the exception of those held in the USA, are not available by country and are therefore included in "Other OECD."

(b) Until 1983-84 Brunei is included in "Other Countries," from 1983-84 it is included in "ASEAN."

(c) Gold held by the Reserve Bank as part of reserve assets which cannot be allocated by country.

n.p. Not available for separate publication (but included in totals where applicable).

Source: Castles, Ian. *Yearbook Australia 1989*. Number 72. Canberra: Australian Bureau of Statistics, 1989.

TABLE 14

Total Australian Aid Flows to Major Recipients 1987-88
Millions of Australian Dollars

Papua New Guinea	306.3
Indonesia	83.5
Malaysia	53.7
China	33.8
Philippines	27.4
Thailand	25.4
Fiji	18.4
Ethiopia	18.3
Bangladesh	14.0
Egypt	14.0
Solomon Islands	11.8
Burma	11.6
Vanuatu	11.1
Mozambique	10.5
Tonga	10.1
Western Samoa	9.8
Hong Kong	9.5
Indo-China Regional	9.1
Vietnam	9.0
Laos	6.9

Sources: Australian International Development Assistance Bureau (AIDAB).

Australian Bureau of Statistics, *Year Book Australia 1989.*

for established natural gas and oil operations. Due to southern Chile's geographic diversity, the area is emerging as the focus of tourism-business development efforts in the early 1990s.

Some Latin American observers believe the 1980s were a "lost decade" due to a burgeoning, mismanaged external debt; rampant inflation which deteriorated living standards; and appreciable per capita income losses. Actually, in view of Latin America's economic performance and economic mismanagement, which deteriorated the aggregate social condition in the 1980s, the 1980s would be more accurately labeled as "the over-extended decade." According to World Bank and Inter-American Development Bank estimates, Latin America's total disbursed short-term debt, long-term debt, and use of IMF credits, surged from $161 billion in 1978 to $441 billion in 1987. By 1988, the total debt figure dropped $15 billion to an estimated $426 billion due in part to debt-to-equity conversion programs in Brazil, Mexico, Chile, and Venezuela. "From 1982, as countries struggled to restructure their debt obligations, a clear shift away from short-term debt became evident. Whereas long-term debt represented less than 72 percent of the total during 1980-82, it reached 88 percent in 1987 as supplier credits and other forms of short-term financing became difficult to obtain."[47]

Initially, Chile's growing contribution to Latin America's external debt situation, accompanied with economic restructuring toward market-oriented policies, assisted an average 7 percent in the GDP growth rate in the 1976-1981 period. Still realigning the economy from the 1973 socialist policy vestiges, Chile's inflation levels contracted substantially while hundreds of nationalized companies were resold to the private sector. Today, the government still owns a variety of companies including oil and copper operations. In fact, CODELCO, a state-owned copper company, along with ENAP and ENAMI, also state-owned enterprises, account for most of the production and employment in Chile.[48]

By 1982, Chile was straddled by burdensome external debt payments and domestic production slowdowns that resulted in rising bankruptcies, high unemployment, and financial deterioration. Amidst a 14 percent GDP drop and a mismanaged external debt burden, Chile agreed to the first of two IMF macroeconomic programs: the first two-year program was agreed to in early 1983 and the next IMF macroeconomic policy coordination agreement of 1985-1988 was extended an additional year. Under these programs capital controls were liberalized, foreign investments were encouraged, tariffs were reduced and export-led growth was pursued along with import substitution. Incentives to raise investment and savings levels were set in motion as well. Employment and stamp taxes were abolished, and VAT and fuel taxes were reduced from 20 to 16 percent. Government current expenditures decreased while capital expenditures expanded; for example, on housing and basic sanitation for the low income sector. Privatization of state owned affiliates of the Production Development Corporation (Corporación de Fomento de Produccion - CORFU) continued to fuel economic growth along with 1987's debt rescheduling which provided for an annual, lower interest rate payment plan instead of a higher-rate, bi-annual repayment schedule. Thanks to these IMF macroeconomic agreements, Chile's economic management maintained stable, pragmatic policies that achieved export-led economic growth; reduced inflation; and strengthened the external sector. In 1987 and 1988, public sector accounts were balanced and price increases were 12.7 percent in 1988 compared to 21.5 percent in 1987. Since the 14 percent 1982 fall in GDP, the GDP figure ranged from 6.3 percent to 2.4 percent in 1984 and 1985, where in 1986 and 1987, the economy grew by 5.7 percent and 5.4 percent, respectively. As for total external debt, the 1985 position of $20.3 billion was drawn down to $16.26 billion in 1989. According to external public debt outstanding in Latin America, Chile ranks sixth behind Brazil, Mexico, Argentina, Venezuela, and Colombia.

In terms of GDP by sector, industry, retail, agriculture, and mining remained the leading contributors. Of the 28 industry subsectors only petroleum and plastics accounted for decreases. Among the fastest growing subsectors were automobiles and vehicles, nonelectrical machinery, glass, office equipment, leather, and soft drinks. Even with restructuring, the industrial sector remains basically under-capitalized, vulnerable to import competition, and burdened by debt. Retail sales rose by 15.4 percent due to enlarged employment opportunities and higher real wages. Due to increased copper and iron production, the mining sector recorded an 8.5 percent gain. Market shares increased in all sectors, relative to monetary values, where ranking positions among the top four sectors (industry, retail, agriculture, and mining) remained the same (Table 15).

TABLE 15

Chile's GDP By Sector 1980-1988
Billions of Constant 1977 Chilean Pesos

	1980	1981	1982	1983	1984	1985	1986	1987	1988*
Agriculture	28	29	28	27	29	31	33	35	37
Fishing	2	2	3	3	3	3	4	4	4
Mining	26	28	30	29	30	31	32	32	33
Industry	78	80	63	65	72	73	78	82	90
Utilities	8	8	8	8	9	9	10	11	11
Construction	19	23	18	17	18	21	21	23	24
Retail	67	70	58	56	59	60	63	67	74
Transport & Commun.	20	21	18	18	19	20	22	23	26
Services	115	122	104	104	109	109	114	121	128
Total	**363**	**383**	**329**	**327**	**348**	**357**	**377**	**398**	**427**

*preliminary

Sources: Central Bank, National Institute of Statistics, and United States Embassy estimates.

Chilean exports range from copper, fruit, basic metals, fishmeal, to paper/cellulose, and timber. Chile is the world's largest producer and exporter of copper. Chile's copper resources and reserves are approximately 20 percent of the world's total. The ore is either processed into electrolytic or blister copper before export. CODELCO is Chile's largest state-owned copper supplier, producing about 1.1 million tons annually. CODELCO possesses 70 percent of the nation's copper reserves and operates the four largest mines: Chuquicamata, El Teniente, Andina, and El Salvador. Copper accounts for about 43 percent of Chilean exports and mineral products totalled 50 percent of exports in 1987 to 48 percent in 1988. Other primary Chilean exports include molybdenum, silver, iron ore, gold, and is one of the largest producers of elemental iodine. From 1984 to 1988, exports of fresh fruits, manufactures, non-copper mining products, and fishery and forest products, grew by 22 percent. To date, Chile ranks as the leading Latin American fish producer. Total fish catch amounts to over 5 million tons among varieties of hake, mackerel, sardine, and anchovy. Timber supplies, primarily fast-growing radiata pine, are used to produce sawn wood and pulp.[49] As for raw timber sales, only Chile and the United States ship unmilled logs in sizeable quantities in the international market. Main Chilean export destinations are the United States, Taiwan, Japan, West Germany, and Italy. Exports from 1978 to 1988 expanded 188 percent.

Major import products include the basic array among modern consumer and capital goods: petroleum, motor vehicles, machinery, electronic equipment, and durables. All imports are subject to a 15 percent across-the-board tariff. The merchandise trade balance has remained positive since 1982 despite increased real earnings given Chile's economic performance. Leading import suppliers comprise the United States, Japan, West Germany, and France. In 1978 to 1988, imports increased 69 percent.

Within the Pacific Rim Region market, Chile's primary importers constitute the United States, Japan, Colombia, Canada, and South Korea. Exports partners vary among the Northeast Quarter and Northwest Quarter with the United States, Japan, Taiwan, South Korea, and China (Table 16).

TABLE 16

Chile's Bilateral Trade With Pacific Rim Region, Selected Members 1978-1988, Millions of United States Dollars

Exports

	1978	1979	1980	1981	1982	1983	1984	1985	1986	1987	1988
Northwest Quarter											
Japan	278	416	507	427	440	348	408	385	420	561	881
South Korea	32	65	70	61	52	57	65	88	92	109	146
China, People's Republic	30	97	105	61	62	93	125	146	100	79	99
Taiwan	31	68	52	70	34	31	45	39	61	130	245
Southwest Quarter											
Australia	1	1	6	6	2	2	4	6	7	17	22
Southeast Quarter											
Ecuador	20	29	22	14	51	34	28	34	28	33	35
Peru	10	20	71	70	49	39	45	46	66	86	63
Northeast Quarter											
Canada	18	28	79	141	34	60	31	76	58	71	48
United States	321	414	589	592	801	1083	951	877	915	1,141	1,393
Mexico	15	44	68	87	22	1	9	51	10	3	24
Costa Rica	....	....	....	....	....	....	....	....	....	6	10
Panama	17	10	11	11	7	4	5	6	7	....	....
Colombia	42	62	77	71	46	42	43	55	41	51	58
Hong Kong	2	2	15	2	8	3	9	10	13	14	46
Malaysia	4	....	....	....	....	4	....	....	....	....	....

TABLE 16 (continued)

Chile's Bilateral Trade With Pacific Rim Region, Selected Members 1978-1988, Millions of United States Dollars

Imports

	1978	1979	1980	1981	1982	1983	1984	1985	1986	1987	1988
Northwest Quarter											
Japan	227	319	370	673	230	161	312	188	296	387	392
South Korea	21	35	30	41	51	23	41	24	48	82	108
China, People's Republic	12	26	21	35	22	10	12	24	21	57	55
Taiwan	37	58	99	147	53	27	37	24	28	55	67
Southwest Quarter											
Australia[1]	2	16	9	9	3	7	8	8	11	15	18
Southeast Quarter											
Ecuador	95	174	210	100	33	40	46	48	59	37	56
Peru	35	53	41	67	38	37	49	41	56	28	33
Northeast Quarter											
Canada	62	79	77	94	56	61	67	59	54	66	111
United States	810	954	1,464	1,632	916	704	748	655	642	773	1,002
Mexico	42	56	28	43	11	17	22	15	20	44	69
Costa Rica											
Panama	10	13	92	109	21	3	1	2	4	3	2
Columbia	21	37	18	26	11	13	22	22	38	100	127
Hong Kong	13	26	30	5	27	14	20	11	16	24	27
Malaysia	5	11	9	....	....	5	11	9	....	....	....

[1] f.o.b.

Source: International Monetary Fund. *Direction of Trade Statistics*. Various Editions: 1989, 1988 and 1984. Washington, D.C.

Chile's foreign trade policy focuses on pursuing an open market policy along with an emphasis on export-led growth. By 1979, import tariffs were a uniform 10 percent until a temporary increase to 35 percent occurred to assist a government revenue shortfall. In July 1985, tariffs were reduced to 20 percent where by January 1988 tariffs leveled out to 15 percent across the board except for a limited number of items such as automobiles, textiles, and innertubes. Through export-led growth, a full integration into the international economy must occur. Similar to the *laissez faire* ideal of the nineteenth century, public sector intervention must be limited where prices and wages are determined through the forces of supply and demand. Also, integral to Chile's success with export-led growth involved extensive use of debt-equity swaps by foreign investors totalling $1.6 billion since 1985. Because of these programs, capital intensive, import substitution industrialization occurred without government subsidies, which has provided Chile access to private international credit markets that otherwise would be unavailable given Chile's burdensome $16.26 billion external debt. With these above conditions, plus the Central Bank exchange rate policy changing from adjusting "the peso for less than internal inflation to one which changes the peg for more than Chilean inflation (thus, making imports more expensive in real terms)," provides the firm foundation for the long-term export-led growth strategy.[50] Since consenting to the 1983 IMF macroeconomic program, the Chilean economy continues to grow through six consecutive years, unemployment levels continue to fall, family real incomes are increasing, and export volumes through 1993 are anticipated to expand by 10-15 percent.

Chile - Exchange Arrangements/Exchange Restrictions

As for Chile's exchange arrangements and exchange restrictions, the December 1988 position varies nominally from the December 1987 position. As reported to the IMF, the Chilean peso is pegged to the United States Dollar. The peso is adjusted at daily intervals with respect to a schedule based on the domestic rate of inflation during the previous month, minus the estimated world inflation rate.[51] Intervention margins of plus-or-minus 3 percent, on either side of the official exchange rate, are maintained through Central Bank intervention. The Central Bank of Chile administers currency exchange policy through the Executive Committee. Within specified rules stipulated by the Central Bank of Chile, the Chilean Copper Commission supervises copper exports and all imports of the copper industry. Within the multilateral clearing system of the Latin American Integration Association (LAIA), accounts with Argentina, Bolivia, Brazil, Colombia, Ecuador, Mexico, Paraguay, Peru, Uruguay, and Venezuela are maintained through the Central Bank of Chile and the central banks of each country concerned. Due to a reciprocal credit agreement with the Dominican Republic, settlement transactions utilize specified clearing accounts. Other countries settle their accounts through designated convertible currencies.

Except for used motor vehicle import permits, imports are primarily unrestricted. In general, all imports are subject to a 15 percent tariff, which usually is offset by a registration tax of up to 3 percent. The 15 percent across-the-board tariff gives way to various GATT and LAIA negotiated tariffs agreements. "Tariff duties or surcharges are applied, on a temporary basis, on imports of certain products that are subsidized in the country of origin."[52] For example, some imports of dairy products such as condensed and powdered milk, butter, and cheese are based on EC internal prices; the market which these imports originated. In order to receive payment for visible trade items, a Central Bank document (*Informe de Importacion*) "must be obtained and processed through the intermediary local commercial bank."[53] Deferred payment terms (*cobertura diferida*) exceeding 360 days require Central Bank approval for imports. Import payments exceeding $20,000 command a 120-day minimum financing requirement.

Restrictions for invisibles include an equivalent of $1,000 for tourist travel, in addition to transportation fares to Latin America and Caribbean nations, and a maximum of $3,000 to other countries. "Residents may purchase up to US$ 200 a month for study abroad, subscriptions to magazines, books, and pension payments, subject to presentation of appropriate documents."[54] Through adequate justification, the Central Bank may increase spending levels for these invisibles.

Exports flow unimpeded from Chile. Foreign exchange earnings exceeding $1,000 must be surrendered through commercial banks. In turn, these banks are required to apprise the Director of Foreign Trade of the Central Bank, or the Chilean Copper Commission with respect to copper sales earnings. "Export proceeds subject to surrender requirements must be repatriated within 90 days from the date of shipment, and surrendered within 10 days. However, export proceeds may be surrendered within 180 days from the date of shipment if they are held as swaps or foreign exchange deposits with resident banks. Extension of repatriation periods may be granted for certain products."[55] Exporters may maintain a Foreign Exchange Account where a yearly balance of $500,000 is permissible within a 2 to 5 percent range of their export proceeds. CODELCO, the state-owned copper enterprise, maintains its own foreign currency account at the Central Bank.

Capital outflows are restricted where inflows are unhindered. "All new foreign borrowing or refinancing of existing credits by commercial banks require prior approval by the Central Bank...lines of credit of up to one-year maturity with foreign correspondents, and short-term loans for domestic relending" are excluded.[56] Whatever level of foreign borrowing is obtained, the Central Bank of Chile must be notified. Foreign capital entering Chile is identified through one of four arrangements. Among these include Article 14 of Decree Number 471. This article states "that capital brought into the country in the form of foreign borrowing (*creditos externos*) must be sold through authorized banks when the investor (individual or corporate, national or foreign) has registered the transaction with the Central Bank."[57] Article 15 of the above decree provides the Central Bank to make exemptions to the general rules. The Foreign Investment Statute serves as an umbrella for long-term investment options through the guidance of the Foreign Investment Committee (FIC). Typical mining projects approved by the FIC usually entail eight-year mining contracts and three-year contracts for other projects. Investment contracts may include a capital repatriation clause allowing repatriation after three years. Most investment projects of less than $5 million may be approved by the Executive Secretary of the FIC. Two tax schemes are available to foreign investors for total corporate earnings: a guaranteed 49.5 percent a year total corporation income tax, or an effective 32.5 percent tax rate similar to a domestic corporation's tax liabilities. As for oil investments, instead of seeking FIC approval, oil venture contracts are awarded through Presidential Decree.

Under the Chilean Compendium of Rules on International Exchange, the fourth category to identify capital flows "regulates purchases of selected Chilean foreign debt instruments abroad at a discount as well as their repatriation."[58] Eligible external debt instruments are payable in foreign currency with a maturity of more than one year, where the debtor may be "the Treasurer, the Central Bank, a public sector entity, the Development Corporation (CORFU), a financial institution, or a private sector resident having a guarantee from a financial institution...upon approval of the Central Bank, the foreign currency obligation is exchanged into a domestic currency obligation, the proceeds of which must be used for direct investment purposes, with the intermediation of a financial institution; special regulations apply to repatriation of such capital as well as to dividend payments."[59]

Chile - Major Investment Trends

Prevalent Chilean investment trends range from privatizing state owned enterprises, debt-to-equity swaps, to specific investment projects and objectives in the mining, hydrocarbons, energy, and agriculture sectors. CORFU oversees the sales of state-owned enterprises. In 1988, privatization revenues almost tallied $200 million. Due to Chile's success, Chile's Latin American neighbors were piqued with the current privatization effort. According to undisclosed government sources, as conveyed by *The Latin America and Caribbean Review*, employees of nine of the twenty-three state companies owned shares in their respective companies. Some employees sold their subsidized shares to larger investors for a rate far exceeding their original purchase price. White collar and middle management employees seemed to hold their shares regardless of the profit margin. On the corporate purchasing level, numerous foreign companies bought and sold shares in Chilean state enterprises through the Santiago stock exchange or through CORFU. In 1988, 68 percent of the state-owned LAN-Chile airline was sold with approximately one-third of the shares to a corporate buyer. CORFU also sought to find share buyers for regional power companies, Edelmag and Edelnor, in the provinces served by these companies, and Australia's Bond Group purchased 30 percent of the shares in a newly privatized telephone company.

Providing access to international capital otherwise unavailable to the Chilean market, debt-to-equity swaps generated a source of liquidity. Since 1985, primarily United States nationals have participated in debt-to-equity conversions. From 1978 through 1987, United States direct investment activity favored petroleum, trade, and other industries (Table 17).

In the mining, hydrocarbons, and energy sectors, numerous projects and successful investment ventures are underway. In 1988, the Australia Broken Hill Propriety, a Japanese consortium directed by Mitsubishi, and Rio Tiuto Zinc, signed Chile's largest investment project at $1.2 billion. The project involves the Escondida mine where the largest proven copper deposit in the world is located. Chile plans to develop its lithium reserves with estimated production levels that could account for 20 percent of world output. Currently engaged with an intensive prospecting and drilling program, the state-owned Empresa Nacional del Petreleo (ENAP) anticipates increasing its 140,000 b/d oil output. Reserves are estimated at approximately 730 million barrels with offshore fields at the Straits of Magellan, the southern mainland, and onshore at Tierra del Fuego. To date, ENAP is the only oil producer in Chile. By 2003, Chile anticipates to totally replace its 30 percent oil import dependency by diversifying its energy demands among its own oil resources, hydro-electric sources, and coal reserves.[60]

Within the agricultural sector, burgeoning export cash crops since 1980 include onions, garlic, apples, table grapes, citrus fruits, pears, avocado, plums, and nuts. Since 1984, fishing revenues expanded rapidly. In fact, Chile is the leading Latin America fish producer and ranks fifth globally behind Japan, the Soviet Union, China, and the United States. Fish varieties include hake, mackerel, sardine, and anchovy. Salmon breeding began in the early 1980s. According to the National Fishing Service, annual fish catches raised from 3.5 million tons in 1981 to 5.7 million tons in 1986 to 4.9 million tons in 1975. Due to ideal climatic and ecological conditions, salmon breeding operations are located in southern Chile. Salmon are only harvested when northern hemisphere unavailabilities occur. Salmon exports of 300 tons in 1985 increased to 1,400 tons in 1987, to approximately 10,000 tons by 1990.[61] Other industrial fish production has grown since 1980 as well (Table 18).

TABLE 17

United States Direct Investment in Chile, 1978-1987 Cumulative Millions of United States Dollars in Book Value

Year	Total[1]	Mining	Petroleum	Manu-facturing[2]	Transport, Communications, Public Utilities	Trade	Other Industries
1978	230	--	--	71	10	51	26
1979	250	5	70	--	--	49	--
1980	536	209	91	--	--	64	--
1981	834	--	91	--	--	64	--
1982	854	a	79	60	--	71	a
1983	108	--	59	-289	a	64	151
1984	46	--	44	-276	a	49	136
1985	85	--	49	-281	a	42	123
1986	193	--	48	-277	a	37	125
1987	224	--	--	-221	a	21	49

1 Due to incomplete data and rounding, total values do not equal the sum of the industries listed here; finance and insurance excluded.

2 Includes food products, chemicals and allied products, primary and fabricated metals, machinery, transportation equipment and other manufacturing.

a) Suppressed to avoid disclosure of data of individual companies.

Source: Wilke, James H. and Ochoa, Enrique, Editors. *Statistical Abstract of Latin America, Volume 27.* Los Angeles: UCLA Latin American Center Publications, 1988.

TABLE 18

Chile's Industrial Fish Production (1000 tons)

	1980	1985	1986	1987
Frozen	14	22	32	42
Canned	38	45	62	70
Fishmeal	572	1,109	1,274	1,073
Oil	111	184	225	172
Total (includes others)	735	1,360	1,594	1,358

Sources: National Fishing Service.

The Economist Intelligence Unit, *Country Profile: Chile.*

United States - The Economic Context and Trade Policy

Accounting for 14 percent of 1988 world trade and 26.2 percent of world output in 1988, the United States economic prominence continues to pervade the second half of the twentieth century. Since the Allies' 1945 World War II victory and the 1944 Bretton Woods agreement creating the IMF and World Bank (which established the United States Dollar as the international standard for currency values, provided a stabilization program for international currencies, and established a development bank to assist nations with domestic development in order to maintain currency values with their own resources), the United States international stature represents a bastion of peace, free trade, and open markets. As the leader of the free world, the United States funded the reconstruction of Europe through the $12 billion Marshall Plan and assisted with Japan's postwar economic development. Today, in terms of production output and international commerce activity, Japan and West Germany rank as the world's second and third largest economies behind the United States.

Technologically, American inventors are renowned for innovative, practical scientific developments. Yet, during the previous ten to fifteen years, American innovations tend to languish domestically while other markets, notably Japan, capitalize on the innovations sooner, and mass produce new innovative technologies before American companies. Most notable technological achievements unique to the United States include six manned lunar landings and a reusable Space Transportation System (STS), commonly known as the Space Shuttle. The space transportation system was designed as an orbital vehicle capable of deploying and retrieving satellites, and conducting in-flight experiments.

Currently, the United States government and manufacturing sectors are beset with management inefficiencies that could be remedied easily with humility, increased expenditures for capital improvements, and the confidence of the United States Congress to realize deficit-spending endangers their constituencies' support. With tax increases looming in the foreseeable future, American citizens will soon pay for the United States government's fiscal mismanagement that ultimately translates into lower constituency support levels. In the manufacturing sector, particularly automobiles, other numerous consumer items, and even the Hubble Space Telescope project, suffer from quality control inadequacies. If one ponders the notion of where American automobile quality, or manufacturing quality in general, would be today without foreign competition, it would truly prove an even more disheartening proposition. By mid-1990, automobile imports comprised 33.3 percent of the American new car market, a new record.

The United States possesses the manufacturing capabilities, management knowledge, and marketing prowess required within today's marketplace. With adequate capital improvements, and realigned management strategies, the United States will successfully resolve its two burdensome deficits: the merchandise trade deficit and budget deficit. Meanwhile, preferring imports over domestic items, and spending more than government receipts earn, continue to enlarge these imbalanced accounts. Providing quality manufactures, and weaning the American people from the nipple of exorbitant government spending, would dramatically reduce, or eliminate, these deficits through effective, practical management. Historically, the United States merchandise trade account shows a continuous deficit since 1976 to date. The 1988 $155.1 billion government budget deficit continues the deficit spending pattern that began in 1969. According to current estimates, the 1990 budget deficit figure may rival or exceed the record 1986 level of $221.2 billion.

Fortunately, due to the United States previous economic and technological track record; stable government structure; sound monetary policy administered by the Federal Reserve System; well-developed domestic infrastructure; diversified economy; abundant natural resources; and the leading position in international assets, economic output and international trade; the United States Dollar maintains its traditional stature as a "safe haven" among international investors. Principal export trading partners are Canada, Japan, West Germany, South Korea, and Mexico. Leading export items include: machinery and transportation equipment; grains and preparations; animal feed; nonmetallic mineral manufactures; and professional, scientific, controlling instruments. On the import side, major United States imports consist of machinery and transport equipment; office machines; road motor vehicles and aircraft equipment; clothing; metal manufactures; and petroleum and related products. Major source countries include Canada, Japan, South Korea, West Germany, and Taiwan. From 1978 to 1988, United States exports expanded 123 percent and imports grew 147 percent. From the Pacific Rim Region context, seventeen Region members, in 1988, placed in the billion dollar importers' category with Japan and Canada earning the largest receipts. Distanced by an easy $55 billion, Taiwan placed third followed by Mexico and South Korea. In 1985, Japanese imports overtook Canadian imports by $2.9 billion and Japan has remained the United States most active importer ever since. As for the export sector, Canada, Japan and Mexico are the strongest markets for American exports. Taiwan, South Korea, and Australia follow with Tonga, Kiribati, Vanuatu, and Laos rounding off the list (Table 19).

TABLE 19

United States Bilateral Trade with Pacific Rim Region, Selected Members 1978-1988, Millions of United States Dollars

Exports

	1978	1979	1980	1981	1982	1983	1984	1985	1986	1987	1988
Northwest Quarter											
Soviet Union	2,283	3,616	1,515	2,432	2,613	2,003	3,284	2,423	1,248	1,480	2,768
Japan	12,885	17,597	20,790	21,823	20,966	21,894	23,575	22,631	26,882	28,249	37,732
North Korea											
South Korea	3,160	4,191	4,685	5,116	5,529	5,925	5,983	5,956	6,355	8,099	11,290
China, People's Republic	824	1,724	3,755	3,603	2,912	2,173	3,004	3,856	3,106	3,497	5,039
Taiwan	2,376	3,380	4,673	4,765	4,563	4,667	5,003	4,700	5,524	7,413	12,131
Hong Kong	1,625	2,083	2688	2,636	2,453	2,563	3,062	2,786	3,030	3,983	5,691
Philippines	1,040	1,570	1,999	1,787	1,854	1,807	1,766	1,379	1,363	1,599	1,880
Laos	1	1	....	....	....	....	....	....	....	....	1
Vietnam	2	1	1	10	32	21	22	20	30	23	15
Kampuchea	....	....	26	12	2	2	1	....	....	....	....
Thailand	629	961	1,263	1,170	915	1,063	1,113	849	936	1,544	1,964
Myanmar	30	32	29	34	34	15	16	10	16	8	11
Malaysia	728	932	1,337	1,537	1,736	1,684	1,856	1,539	1,730	1,897	2,139
Singapore	1,462	2,331	3,033	3,003	3,214	3,759	3,675	3,476	3,380	4,053	5,770
Brunei	35	51	70	45	79	58	34	51	202	93	78
Southwest Quarter											
Indonesia	751	981	1,545	1,302	2,025	1,466	1,217	795	946	767	1,056
Papua New Guinea	32	33	38	55	66	84	53	41	51	51	113
Australia	2,910	3,617	4,093	5,242	4,534	3,954	4,793	5,440	5,551	5,495	6,981
New Zealand	405	530	595	922	897	620	708	728	881	819	942
Solomon Islands	....	....	....	....	....	....	....	....	....	8	5
Fiji	....	....	....	....	....	....	....	....	....	....	15

TABLE 19 (continued)

United States Bilateral Trade with Pacific Rim Region, Selected Members 1978-1988, Millions of United States Dollars

Exports

	1978	1979	1980	1981	1982	1983	1984	1985	1986	1987	1988
Southwest Quarter (continued)											
New Caledonia	....	....	....	....	....	....	....	....	....	28	27
Tonga	....	....	....	....	....	....	....	....	....	....	4
Vanuatu	....	....	....	....	....	....	....	....	....	....	2
Nauru	....	....	....	....	....	....	....	....	....	6	....
Kiribati	....	....	....	....	....	....	....	....	....	....	3
Southeast Quarter											
Ecuador	610	696	864	854	828	597	655	591	601	621	684
Peru	501	720	1,172	1,486	1,117	900	751	496	693	814	798
Chile	725	885	1,354	1,465	925	729	805	682	824	796	1,065
Western Samoa	4	3	4	18	3	5	4	2	2	3	4
French Polynesia	51	59	....	23	22	29	7	....	6	2	87
Northeast Quarter											
Canada	28,372	33,096	35,395	39,564	33,720	38,224	46,524	47,251	45,333	59,814	69,233
Mexico	6,680	9,958	15,146	17,789	11,817	9,082	11,992	13,635	12,392	14,582	20,643
Guatemala	398	467	553	559	390	316	377	405	400	480	591
Honduras	288	324	379	349	275	299	322	308	363	418	478
El Salvador	366	352	273	308	292	365	426	446	518	390	483
Nicaragua	184	100	250	184	119	132	112	42	3	3	6
Costa Rica	335	413	498	373	330	382	423	422	483	582	696
Panama	438	527	699	844	845	748	757	675	712	742	633
Colombia	1,046	1,409	1,736	1,771	1,903	1,514	1,450	1,468	1,319	1,412	1,758

TABLE 19 (continued)

United States Bilateral Trade with Pacific Rim Region, Selected Members 1978-1988, Millions of United States Dollars

Imports

	1978	1979	1980	1981	1982	1983	1984	1985	1986	1987	1988
Northwest Quarter											
Soviet Union	563	907	486	377	247	375	600	443	606	470	649
Japan	26,471	28,173	32,973	39,904	39,931	43,559	60,371	72,380	85,457	88,074	93,168
North Korea											
South Korea	4,087	4,349	4,433	5,474	6,011	7,657	10,027	10,713	13,497	17,991	21,209
China, People's Republic	357	656	1,164	2,062	2,502	2,477	3,381	4,224	5,241	6,910	9,270
Taiwan	5,010	5,652	6,760	8,158	8,757	12,110	16,088	17,761	21,251	26,406	26,256
Hong Kong	3,767	4,307	5,029	5,758	5,895	6,825	8,899	8,994	9,474	10,490	10,810
Philippines	1,346	1,648	1,913	2,161	1,956	2,160	2,622	2,334	2,150	2,481	2,906
Laos	1	2	1	1	2	3	2	1	....	1	3
Vietnam	....	....	1	....	....	....	....	....	....	....	....
Kampuchea	....	....	....	1	....	....	....	....	1	....	....
Thailand	478	646	866	1,007	956	1,035	1,426	1,543	1,873	2,387	3,424
Myanmar	4	13	9	16	18	12	15	15	15	13	13
Malaysia	1,596	2,252	2,688	2,272	1,959	2,205	2,825	2,399	2,534	3,053	3,853
Singapore	1,119	1,535	1,985	2,195	2,274	2,969	4,121	4,412	4,884	6,395	8,226
Brunei	162	185	293	343	219	20	11	2	64	17	30
Southwest Quarter											
Indonesia	3,906	3,927	5,539	6,413	4,509	5,6t7	5,867	4,933	3,675	3,719	3,494
Papua New Guinea	74	75	57	55	19	27	29	36	48	23	36
Australia	1,854	2,387	2,782	2,707	2,552	2,422	2,899	3,067	2,873	3,287	3,856
New Zealand	605	794	793	820	870	828	880	969	1,097	1,181	1,303
Solomon Islands	....	....	....	....	....	....	....	....	....	....	3

TABLE 19 (continued)

United States Bilateral Trade with Pacific Rim Region, Selected Members 1978-1988, Millions of United States Dollars

Imports

	1978	1979	1980	1981	1982	1983	1984	1985	1986	1987	1988
Southwest Quarter (continued)											
Fiji	....	....	....	....	....	....	....	....	....	....	14
New Caledonia	....	....	....	....	....	....	....	....	....	....	34
Tonga	....	....	....	....	....	....	....	....	....	....	1
Vanuatu	....	....	....	....	....	....	....	....	....	....	8
Nauru	3	....	....	....	....	....	....	....	....	....	....
Kiribati	....	....	....	....	....	....	....	....	....	....	2
Southeast Quarter											
Ecuador	810	909	953	1,103	1,227	1,520	1,804	1,975	1,603	1,390	1,370
Peru	694	1,258	1,443	1,277	1,150	1,204	1,402	1,152	858	815	701
Chile	421	482	559	661	729	1,053	871	858	935	1,105	1,326
Western Samoa	1	2	2	2	3	8	7	25	2	2	2
French Polynesia	70	115	....	4	4	4	....	....	1	1	11
Northeast Quarter											
Canada	34,647	38,970	41,999	46,827	46,792	52,546	66,911	69,427	68,662	71,510	81,434
Mexico	6,195	8,997	12,835	4,013	15,770	17,019	18,267	19,392	17,558	20,520	23,545
Guatemala	362	437	465	384	365	404	479	448	647	542	477
Honduras	380	469	475	493	426	435	450	433	487	565	576
El Salvador	302	459	444	270	333	362	406	413	401	300	299
Nicaragua	227	251	227	152	98	109	69	50	1	1	1
Costa Rica	334	437	405	426	421	453	544	570	720	750	861
Panama	174	223	353	329	289	378	365	467	412	402	297
Colombia	1,105	1,289	1,327	900	883	1,058	1,253	1,456	2,039	2,414	2,349

Source: International Monetary Fund. *Direction of Trade Statistics*. Various Editions: 1989, 1988 and 1984. Washington, D.C.

Despite relatively few domestic protection measures and few politically motivated trade restrictions, the United States espouses free trade and open markets. The farm sector and the textiles industry are well protected in the United States, with trade restrictions applying to North Korea, Vietnam, Kampuchea, Iran, Libya, and Cuba. Also, due to the 2 August 1990 incursion, occupation, and subsequent liberation of Kuwait, trade restrictions are in effect for Iraq at this writing. In its commitment to counter protectionism, the United States Administration has placed the multilateral trade regulations in the Uruguay Round as priority in trade policy.

Throughout the 1980s, protectionist currents culminated with the passage of the Omnibus Trade and Competitiveness Act of 1988. From failed voluntary export restraints of Japanese cars to successive renewals of the Multifiber Arrangement (MFA), which corresponds growth of imports to domestic sales, and the trigger price mechanism for steel imports instead of voluntary export arrangements, engendered the Trade and Tariff Act of 1984 and the Omnibus Trade and Competitiveness Act of 1988. Strengthened retaliatory authority was extended to the President through the Trade and Tariff Act of 1984 as well as the authority to negotiate bilateral and multilateral trade arrangements. By 1988, the Omnibus Trade and Competitiveness Act provided the President with a "fast-track" authority to seek protective measures for agricultural, services, and intellectual property rights protection. Also, included, is the "Super-301" clause that requires the US Trade Representative to specifically "identify barriers to trade and investment of priority interest to the United States, based upon an annual National Trade Estimates Report."[62] The "Special-301" involves unfair trading with respect to intellectual property rights, where losses of $24 billion occurred in 1986 according to the United States International Trade Commission.[63] As stipulated by "Super-301," Brazil, Japan, and India received the first honors under this clause. "Special-301" requirements avoided listing specific countries and a priority watch list mentioned Brazil, Mexico, Saudi Arabia, China, South Korea, Taiwan, and Thailand.[64] Among an array of categories, the Omnibus Act also created a National Advisory Committee on Semiconductors, which will assist United States leadership in the industry through development and applications of semiconducting. High-temperature superconductivity (HTS) and high-definition television (HDTV) were specifically referred to in the Omnibus Act.

In an effort to realign the United States and Japan's bilateral $49 billion trade imbalance, the United States initiated the Structural Impediment Initiative (SII) talks during June 1989. Although an agreement was reached in July 1990, Congressional approval is required before SII becomes policy. Since negotiators agreed to maintain the SII discussions indefinitely, with regular meetings and annual reports for the next three years, it proves advantageous to include SII as a United States trade policy point. SII proposals agreed to by Japan include toughening its antitrust policies, streamlining its distribution system, and investing more on public works. The United States consented to a variety of proposals that include increasing research and development spending, balancing its budget, and boosting worker training.[65]

Another dimension of United States trade policy concerns the Enterprise for the Americas Initiative. Still in the initial stages, the Enterprise for the Americas calls for substantial trade, investment, and debt initiatives for Latin America. Proposed in June 1990, this new initiative envisions a free-trade zone for the entire Western Hemisphere. Through close cooperation among Latin American markets, bilateral agreements will form the foundation toward a Western Hemisphere free-trade zone. In those countries unprepared for free-trade agreements, closer trade relations will be negotiated. In a motion to encourage investment in Latin America, the United States will contribute $100 million annually (for five years) to a proposed $300 million fund to be administered by the Inter-American Development Bank to promote privatization and market-oriented reforms. The United States will seek matching funds from Western Europe and Japan. As for debt reduction, the United States government will pursue up to 50 percent write-offs for the $7 billion outstanding in below market rate loans among United States government agencies. Write-offs, or write-downs, would be limited to those economies engaged in IMF or World Bank "approved economic policies and have concluded debt reduction programs with commercial creditor banks."[66] Of the $5 billion market rate loans held by the United States government, an undisclosed portion would be sold to assist debt-for-equity and debt-for-nature exchanges. For some conservation projects, local currencies would be considered for interest payments where interest payments on renegotiated loans would be considered for funding conservation projects.[67]

The United States also encourages trade relations through the Generalized System of Preferences (GSP) and the Caribbean Basin Initiative (CBI). In general, each program provides preferred treatment with respect to import duties and a most favored nation status. Each program will be further discussed in the following Exchange Arrangements and Exchange Restrictions section.

To encourage export activity, the Export-Import Bank of the United States (Eximbank) provides assistance and aid in financing exports of United States goods and services. Established in February 1934, the Export-Import Bank of Washington became an independent agency in 1945, and a name change occurred in 1968 to Eximbank. Eximbank will consider assisting export financing of United States goods and services providing private sector funding is unavailable and repayment is reasonably assured. Eximbank is authorized to have a capital stock of $1 billion and the ability to borrow from the United States Treasury to an amount of $6 billion at any one time. Eximbank's total exposure limit at any one time is $40 billion among aggregate dollar loans, guarantees, and insurance. Since 1987, Eximbank primarily offers one loan program and one guarantee program for medium-term and long-term export transactions. Eighty-five percent financing is available for each program on the basis of preliminary and final commitments, and are open to any responsible party. "Eximbank loans also carry the maximum interest rate allowed by the Organization for Economic Cooperation and Development. Other changes, including a restructuring of fee schedules based on risk, will help make Eximbank programs more accessible to financial institutions and to exporters."[68]

Eximbank also offers export credit insurance programs, which reduce the risk of buyer default. The Foreign Credit Insurance Association (FCIA), an association of United States insurance companies, has administered these programs since 1961. The FCIA, or the Association, sells and services export credit insurance coverage through agreements with Eximbank. In the event FCIA policies are unable to meet specific exporting insurance requirements, insurance plans that tailor to the special needs of exporters and financial institutions are available. Other Eximbank programs, such as the Working Capital Guarantee Program and the Engineer Multiplier

Program, offer loan guarantees to lenders extending working capital loans to exporters, and financing for projects related to design services or feasibility studies with a prospect of generating further American exports, respectively.[69]

United States - Exchange Arrangements/Exchange Restrictions

As reported in the IMF, *Exchange Arrangements and Exchange Restrictions Annual Report 1989*, United States highlights are among administration, imports, exports, and rudimentary capital flow regulations. United States Dollar values are based on the forces of supply and demand for spot and forward exchange rates in the exchange markets. Taxes on subsidies, with respect to United States Dollar foreign exchange transactions, are nonexistent. According to the Cuban Assets Control Regulations, the Foreign Assets Control Regulations, and the Libyan Sanctions Regulations, the Department of Treasury administers licensing programs for direct or indirect financial or commercial transactions with Cuba, the People's Republic of Kampuchea, the Democratic People's Republic of Korea, the Socialist Republic of Vietnam, the Socialistic People's Libyan Arab Jamahiriya, and their nationals. Also administered by the Department of Treasury are blocked accounts of Estonia, East Germany, Latvia, and Lithuania, as prescribed by the Foreign Funds Control Regulations since World War II. South African trade and investment sanctions, prohibiting specified trade and investment activities, corresponds to the South African Transactions Regulations as designated by the Comprehensive Anti- Apartheid Act of 1986. Various agencies administer import and export quotas which the Customs Service of the Treasury Department, the Department of Agriculture, and the Department of Commerce serve distinct objectives. The Department of Agriculture regulates particular import quotas for dairy products, and the Department of Commerce imposes export quotas for munitions items. Global quotas for sugar and sugar products are set by the Secretary of Agriculture on an annual basis.

In terms of imports, quotas are maintained for a variety of products that include cotton, certain cotton waste and products, most dairy products, peanuts, sugar and certain sugar products, and certain specialty steel products. Except for peanuts, certain cotton products, butter, butter oil, certain other dairy products, and certain sugar products, quantitative import quotas are considered on a country of production basis. Within the parameters of GATT, the Multifiber Arrangement, thirty bilateral restraints agreements, and twelve agreements with nonsignators of the MFA, textile and apparel exports to the United States will continue "while minimizing the disruption of the United States markets for these products."[70] These imports are monitored along with their impacts upon the domestic textile and apparel industries. If conditions prove adverse to the above agreements, consultations and new trade guidelines will amend the situation.

Since January 1976, duty-free imports from the Generalized System of Preferences expanded from \$3.2 billion to \$18.4 billion in December 1988. In effect through 4 July 1993, the GSP provides for "product graduation" that allows duty-free treatment until a particular product can be withdrawn "in which the beneficiary country becomes competitive. Cumulative treatment under the GSP scheme is extended to beneficiary members of the Andean Group, ASEAN, and CARICOM; accumulation allows two or more countries of an eligible association to contribute jointly to the requirement that at least 35 percent of the direct cost of producing a given product should originate in the beneficiary country. Exempted from competitive needs limits is a category of countries designated as 'least-developed' beneficiaries" which range from Bangladesh, The Gambia, Maldives, to the Yemen Arab Republic.[71] Other preferential import programs include the Free Trade Agreements with Israel and Canada.

In the export sector, as mentioned earlier, munitions exports are regulated through licensing by the Department of Commerce. Excluding members of the North Atlantic Treaty Organization (NATO), Japan, Australia, and New Zealand, crime control equipment, detection equipment, along with related technical data and pertinent instruments, are regulated through the Department of Commerce. The Commerce Department also administers controls on exports and re-exports. For the sake of ongoing market assessments, export companies are required to report export activity figures for numerous commodities: wheat, flour, rice, corn, sorghum, cotton, soybeans and soybean products, and others. Generally, export and import activity from and to the United States is considered unrestrictive except for the above conditions.

Capital flows through the United States are unimpeded with exceptions to the nations listed on page 102. Amounts of $10,000 in cash or negotiable instruments must be declared upon entering or leaving the United States. Foreigners who own five percent or more of United States agricultural land must report their participation to the United States Department of Agriculture. Although loans, extension of credit, and demand deposits from South Africa are prohibited, trade credits are permissible.

International Banking Facilities (IBFs), as of 3 December 1981, established operations in the United States. Comprised of United States chartered depository institutions, United States offices of Edge Act and Agreement Corporations, and United States branches and agencies of foreign banks, IBFs accept deposits only "from foreign residents (including foreign offices of domestic banks), from other IBFs, or from the institution establishing the IBF."[72] For nonbank foreign residents, the minimum transaction amount is $100,000 and the minimum maturity notice requirement is two business days. "Funds raised by an IBF may be used only to extend credit to foreign residents (including foreign officers of domestic banks), to other IBFs, or to the entity establishing the IBF. Credit may be extended to nonbank foreign residents only if the proceeds are used to finance operations of the borrower or its affiliates outside the United States. Advances from an IBF to its establishing entity in the United States are subject to Eurocurrency reserve requirements in the same manner as advances to the establishing entity from the entity's foreign offices."[73] IBFs are exempt from Federal Deposit Insurance Corporation insurance coverage and assessments, and numerous states have extended favorable tax benefits to IBF operations.

United States - Major Investment Trends

Numerous investment trends such as substantial defense spending, an income earning emphasis shift from the manufacturing sector to services, a burgeoning government budget deficit, the savings and loans failures, and direct investment activities prevailed in the United States during the 1978-1988 period. Since 1983, the United States embarked upon the longest peace-time expansion on record, fueled in part by favorable energy prices, government defense spending, and related economic activity required to service these trends. Starting at $176.53 billion in 1982, defense spending increased to $243.74 billion in 1985, and peaked in 1988 at $277.99 billion. Even with impressive defense funding, excluding defense research and development, United States research and development (R&D) is only two- thirds the amount spent in Japan and West Germany as a percentage of GNP. In some circles, observers believe the United States is allowing its technological advantage to slide by. In absolute dollar terms, in 1989, United States R&D amounted to $65.2 billion compared to $26.3 billion in Japan and $11.4 billion in West Germany, according to Standard and Poor's Compustat Services.[74] Although far from a definitive account of R&D research levels, these numbers, in comparison to mid-1980 levels, serve as indicators rather than accurate non-defense R&D expenditures. As for percentages to GNP, these can be deceiving since, in absolute terms, the United States GNP far exceeds Japan's and West Germany's GNP figures by $3,105.9 billion and $3,124.3 billion in 1988, respectively.[75] The crux of the situation rests with the United States slow reaction to commercializing an innovative idea before competing nations beat them to the marketplace. For example, foreign markets outpaced United States innovations with cheaper, more powerful semiconductors, digital-audio technologies, and may outpace the United States to the marketplace with high-temperature superconductivity principles and, possibly, fusion operated devices.

The United States maintains the lowest per capita savings rate in the developed world accompanied with the federal government's dis-savings and exorbitant spending. Consequently, the United States government has been unable to balance domestic and international accounts. From an international perspective, since foreigners own more in United States assets than Americans own abroad, the resulting balance classifies the United States as a net debtor nation. In 1983, the United States was the largest creditor nation with an $89 billion surplus. Burdened by excessive spending, and borrowing to cover these new expenses, the United States became a net debtor nation for the first time in seventy-one years by 1985. In 1988, foreign holdings amounted to $1.79 trillion where total American investments abroad totalled $1.25 trillion.

Throughout the 1980s, a prolonged period of relatively rapid output and productivity growth occurred, while the gist of investment spending occurred in the service sector industries; on information technology which depreciates relatively quickly and where returns are difficult to quantify.[76] Through 1983-86, consumer- led growth reflected strong import performance among an array of consumer goods, where two-thirds of total imports accounted for manufactured goods compared to less than 45 percent ten years ago. Exports tallied 60 percent of manufactured goods and more than half of this percentage were capital goods. Consumer goods showed a small percentage share of exports. Also, during the 1980s, the non-financial corporate sector retired equity and raised fixed interest debt to maximize their cash position or to acquire larger holdings. Bonds in total borrowing doubled since 1985 to 60 percent, and debt to net worth ratios increased over 50 percent from 30 percent in the early 1980s.[77] With increasing debt servicing obligations, and the absence of a substantial increase "in the capacity to produce through new investment, corporate credit quality has eroded."[78]

In terms of the federal government budget deficit, continuous imbalances occurred since 1970 with a $59.2 billion deficit in 1978 and a record $221.2 billion shortfall in 1986. By 1987, interest on the public debt amounted to almost 20 percent of federal outlays or $195.4 billion. As of February 1989, the total national debt amounted to $2.7 trillion. Divided equally among United States families, currently each family's portion amounts to $42,000. Meanwhile, the total deficit is expanding at a rate of approximately $480,000 per minute.[79] Though the Gramm - Rudman - Hollings legislation provides automatic budget cuts toward a balanced budget by 1993, tactics as including the Social Security Trust funds among the government's total assets tend to distort the actual budget balancing process.

Within the financial sector, in the 1970s, savings and loans (S&Ls) started losing depositors since interest paid by banks and other financial institutions exceeded the federally imposed rate ceiling for thrift institutions. Coupled with the low-interest, thirty-year mortgage loans on the books, the S&L industry suffered. With deregulation, S&Ls were permitted to enlarge their lending portfolio parameters which included more risky commercial real estate loans. Buffered by the now broke Federal Savings and Loan Insurance Corporation (FSLIC), unscrupulous and/or high-risk lending activity pervaded the savings and loans' 1980s lending spree. Fueled by sunbelt growth particularly in the Southwest, Texas, and Arizona, laid claim to the majority of failed S&Ls. Bail-out figures for the savings and loans industry range from $325 billion to $1.36 trillion. Based on reports of the Office of Management and Budget, the General Accounting Office, and the United States League of Savings Institutions, costs will approach $456.3 billion over a ten-year period ending in 1999. The accounting office, the investigative arm of Congress, anticipates the bail-out to total $325 billion to $500 billion over the next three decades. *The Stanford Review*, published by Stanford University, projects an estimated cost to $1.369 trillion, by extending the costs over 40 years since the rescue is financed with 30 to 40 year bonds.[80]

Although challenged with federal budget imbalances and the savings and loans industry items, United States economic diversity and political stability continue to attract, generate, and maintain the world's largest direct investment position in the United States and abroad. Direct investment activity in the United States soared 383 percent from $83 billion in 1980 to $401 billion in 1989. Europe, the European Communities, and Japan ranked as the largest investors in the United States with the Middle East and Other Africa, Asia, and Pacific rounding off the list (Table 20). With respect to specific country investment positions in the United States in 1989, the United Kingdom led the group with $119.1 billion, outdistancing Japan by $49.4 billion. The remaining top investors constitute: the Netherlands, $60.5 billion; West Germany, $28.2 billion; Switzerland, $19.3 billion; France, $16.4 billion; Sweden, $4.9 billion; and Belgium, $4.5 billion. Manufacturing and Wholesale Trade remained the dominant industries among foreign investors, although the Petroleum industry gave way to the Other Industries category in the 1982-89 period, where the Real Estate industry maintained its fourth position ranking throughout the same period (Table 21). Other industries are defined as: agriculture, forestry and fishing; construction; transportation; communications and public utilities; motion pictures, television, tape and film; engineering, architectural and surveying services; along with an array of services from advertising to services, nec (not elsewhere classified), provided on a commercial basis.

Within the Pacific Rim Region, leading investors in the United States are Japan, Canada, Australia, Panama, and Singapore.

TABLE 20

Foreign Direct Investment Position in the United States, Selected Countries and Geographic Regions, Yearend 1980-1989
Millions of United States Dollars

	1980	1981	1982	1983	1984	1985	1986	1987	1988	1989
All Countries	83,046	108,714	124,677	137,0611	64,583	184,615	220,414	271,788	328,850	400,817
Canada	12,164	12,116	11,708	11,434	15,286	17,131	20,318	24,013	27,361	31,538
Europe	54,688	72,377	83,193	92,936	108,211	121,413	144,181	186,076	216,418	262,011
European Communities (10)	47,107	64,145	74,012	82,286	96,555	107,105	126,853	164,969	193,301	234,120
European Communities (12)	----	----	----	----	----	----	127,221	165,427	193,912	234,794
Other Europe	7,582	8,232	9,181	10,650	11,655	14,308	17,328	21,107	23,116	27,891
Japan	4,723	7,297	9,677	11,336	16,044	19,313	26,824	35,151	53,354	69,699
Australia, New Zealand, South Africa	428	686	836	999	2,152	3,324	5,634	6,552	5,624	6,532
Latin America and other Western Hemisphere	9,678	11,739	14,229	15,035	16,201	16,826	16,763	12,671	17,019	20,348
Middle East	916	3,588	4,401	4,446	5,336	4,954	4,870	4,998	5,831	6,425
Other Africa, Asia and Pacific	450	511	634	875	1,353	1,654	1,823	2,325	3,243	4,263

Source: United States Department of Commerce, Bureau of Economic Analysis, Washington, D.C.

TABLE 21

Foreign Direct Investment Position in the United States, By Industry, Yearend 1982-1989
Millions of United States Dollars

	1982	1983	1984	1985	1986	1987	1988	1989
All Industries	124,677	137,061	164,583	184,615	220,414	271,788	328,850	400,817
Mining	1,876	1,928	3,920	4,039	5,080	5,718	6,390	7,179
Petroleum	17,660	18,209	25,400	28,270	29,094	35,598	34,704	35,089
Manufacturing	44,065	47,665	51,802	59,584	71,963	94,745	121,434	160,216
Wholesale Trade	18,397	21,031	24,455	29,051	33,997	39,754	50,160	54,549
Retail Trade	5,207	5,482	6,764	6,822	8,923	10,255	14,770	16,802
Banking	7,846	8,697	10,326	11,377	12,394	14,455	17,453	19,581
Finance, Except Banking	2,159	2,269	5,633	4,246	7,239	3,828	2,124	11,403
Insurance	7,928	8,665	8,922	11,806	15,345	17,392	20,252	22,713
Real Estate	11,520	14,636	17,761	19,402	22,512	27,516	31,929	35,853
Other Industries	8,019	8,478	9,599	10,019	13,868	22,527	29,635	37,432

Source: United States Department of Commerce, Bureau of Economic Analysis, Washington, D.C.

Indonesia's United States holdings surged over 377 percent from 1982 to 1989 and China's investment position expanded forty-fold in the same period. Thailand's investment multiplied almost twelve-fold, with comparatively impressive gains below multiples of twenty by Hong Kong, Taiwan, Japan, and Chile in the 1980-1989 period (Table 22).

United States direct investment abroad by industry clearly continued to favor the manufacturing and petroleum sectors. Since 1982, the Finance, Insurance, and Real Estate sector classifications exchanged the number three ranking with Wholesale Trade by 1989. In the Services industry, the investment level, relative to other industry rankings, has remained unchanged from 1982 to 1989, totalling $8.8 billion (Table 23). Most United States foreign investment was directed to Europe, the European Communities, Latin America and other Western Hemisphere nations, including Canada. Throughout 1982-89, African investments and Middle Eastern positions remained relatively consistent except for a 1984 surge of $574 million in the Middle East (Table 24). With respect to the Pacific Rim Region, Canada, Japan and Australia are the only billion-dollar, double-digit recipients of United States direct investment abroad. Within the single digit, billion-dollar category, Panama, Mexico, Hong Kong, Indonesia, and Singapore are the next favored destinations for American investments. In 1982-1989, Nicaraguan investments and China investments surged seven-fold, where Chilean investments increased three-fold, as did Japan, Taiwan, and Papua New Guinea commitments. Panama, New Zealand, and Thailand investment commitments almost doubled from 1982-89, where United States direct investment activity in South Korea almost tripled. As for El Salvador, Guatemala, and Peru, United States private investment positions were reduced (Table 25).

In view of the four predominant markets within the Pacific Rim Region framework, the following multilateral organization will coordinate and operationalize the Pacific Rim Region's inclusive concept into practical use for the private and public sectors.

TABLE 22

Foreign Direct Investment Position in the United States, Selected Countries Pacific Rim Region Members, Yearend 1980-1989 Millions of United States Dollars

	1980	1981	1982	1983	1984	1985	1986	1987	1988	1989
Northwest Quarter										
Japan	4,723	7,697	9,677	11,336	16,044	19,313	26,824	35,151	53,354	69,699
South Korea	-134	-103	-55	-57	-81	-101	383	192	456	-216
China, People's Republic	2	6	D	-7	7	8	10	452	34	83
Taiwan	61	74	80	69	70	107	177	207	329	620
Hong Kong	148	169	229	324	659	640	605	944	892	1,198
Philippines	73	77	102	116	121	118	113	121	140	158
Laos	2	1	1	*	-1	-3	-4	-5	D	D
Kampuchea	0	0	0	0	0	0	0	0	0	-3
Thailand	6	7	7	6	18	13	14	60	55	71
Malaysia	16	21	14	22	22	16	39	9	84	50
Singapore	93	26	97	186	208	242	169	398	475	1,216
Brunei	D	D	D	2	0	0	0	*	0	0
Southwest Quarter										
Indonesia	-1	-2	-5	-2	15	49	37	43	D	377
Australia	338	572	730	930	2,125	3,264	5,466	6,015	5,330	6,236
New Zealand	74	98	96	98	52	72	97	272	213	237
Fiji	D	2	3	3	3	4	9	12	11	5
Vanuatu	*	*	*	*	*	*	*	*	*	
Nauru	0	*	D	D	D	D	D	D	D	D
Southeast Quarter										
Ecuador	7	D	26	32	35	41	45	4	4	3
Peru	*	-3	0	3	3	4	D	6	7	8
Chile	6	-22	-12	3	-5	16	14	26	29	16
French Polynesia	0	*	*	*	*	*	2	2	2	2

TABLE 22 (continued)

Foreign Direct Investment Position in the United States, Selected Countries Pacific Rim Region Members, Yearend 1980-1989 Millions of United States Dollars

	1980	1981	1982	1983	1984	1985	1986	1987	1988	1989
Northeast Quarter										
Canada	12,162	12,116	11,708	11,434	15,286	17,131	20,318	24,013	27,361	31,538
Mexico	136	163	259	244	308	533	847	903	858	958
Guatemala	7	5	2	2	7	8	8	6	7	3
Honduras	4	5	5	6	6	6	6	5	5	5
El Salvador	D	D	12	D	D	D	D	*	1	2
Nicaragua	*	-1	-1	*	*	1	1	2	2	3
Costa Rica	*	*	-1	*	*	*	*	-1	-1	*
Panama	811	913	2,168	2,073	1,924	2,204	2,202	2,319	2,747	2,955
Colombia	29	36	51	63	69	75	78	75	73	58

* Less than $500,000 (+, -)
D Suppressed to avoid disclosure of data of individual companies

Source: United States Department of Commerce, Bureau of Economic Analysis, Washington, D.C.

TABLE 23

United States Direct Investment Position Abroad, By Industry, Yearend 1982-1989
Millions of United States Dollars

	1982	1983	1984	1985	1986	1987	1988	1989
All Industries	207,752	207,203	211,480	230,250	259,800	314,307	333,501	373,436
Mining	1,876	1,928	3,920	4,039	5,080	5,718	6,390	7,179
Petroleum	57,817	57,574	58,051	57,695	58,497	59,774	57,745	57,945
Oil and Gas Extraction	26,027	28,930	30,222	31,366	30,681	32,223	30,496	30,260
Petroleum and Coal Products	19,085	17,211	17,211	16,465	16,383	17,638	17,571	117,671
Petroleum Wholesale Trade	10,835	9,434	8,801	8,048	9,554	8,365	8,026	8,179
Other Petroleum	1,870	1,998	1,807	1,816	1,879	1,548	1,652	1,836
Manufacturing	83,452	82,907	85,865	94,700	105,101	131,645	139,584	155,704
Food and Kindred Products	7,630	7,661	8,156	9,252	11,366	12,682	13,279	15,783
Chemicals and Allied Products	18,274	18,788	19,200	20,273	22,653	27,789	31,922	36,157
Primary and Fabricated Metals	5,463	4,974	5,256	5,012	5,542	6,279	7,856	8,194
Machinery, Except Electrical	13,840	14,294	14,816	18,987	22,090	27,766	26,754	27,137
Electric and Electronic Equipment	7,292	7,328	8,193	8,515	7,049	10,055	10,641	11,872
Transportation Equipment	10,968	10,512	10,664	11,719	13,985	18,752	19,499	23,480
Other Manufacturing	19,985	19,350	19,581	20,942	22,416	28,323	29,634	33,081
Wholesale Trade	20,788	21,278	21,117	22,790	26,214	31,847	33,812	37,735
Banking	10,317	12,387	13,516	14,461	14,510	18,027	19,072	19,875
Finance (Except Banking), Insurance, and Real Estate	18,018	15,075	15,683	22,501	36,414	53,046	60,477	77,112
Services	4,615	4,670	4,447	4,683	5,128	6,706	7,786	8,812
Other Industries	12,745	13,312	12,799	13,421	13,935	13,262	15,025	16,253

Source: United States Department of Commerce, Bureau of Economic Analysis, Washington, D.C.

TABLE 24

United States Direct Investment Position Abroad, Selected Countries and Geographic Regions, Yearend 1982-1989 Millions of United States Dollars

	1982	1983	1984	1985	1986	1987	1988	1989
All Countries	207,752	207,203	211,480	230,250	259,800	314,307	333,501	373,436
Developed Countries	154,3811	155,736	157,123	172,058	194,280	237,508	252,757	279,310
Canada	43,511	44,339	46,730	46,909	50,629	57,783	62,610	66,856
Europe	92,449	92,178	91,589	105,171	120,724	150,439	156,932	176,736
European Communities (10)	71,712	70,210	69,500	81,380	95,629	119,428	125,590	143,360
European Communities (12)	0	0	0	0	98,624	123,999	131,115	149,975
Other Europe	20,737	21,968	22,089	23,791	25,095	31,000	31,342	33,375
Japan	6,407	7,661	7,936	9,235	11,472	15,684	17,927	19,341
Australia, New Zealand, South Africa	12,104	11,558	10,868	10,743	11,455	13,603	15,288	16,377
Developing Countries	48,058	45,746	49,153	52,764	61,072	73,017	77,560	90,552
Latin America and Other Western Hemisphere	28,161	24,133	24,627	28,261	36,851	47,551	51,041	61,364
Other Africa	4,205	4,123	4,456	4,467	3,999	4,372	4,199	4,310
Saharan Africa	1,573	1,853	2,037	2,423	2,115	2,092	2,065	2,235
Sub-Saharan Africa	2,632	2,270	2,420	2,074	1,884	2,280	2,134	2,076
Middle East	3,550	4,451	5,025	4,606	4,891	4,084	3,806	3,886
Other Asia and Pacific	12,142	13,039	15,045	15,400	15,332	17,010	18,515	20,991
OPEC[1]	8,081	8,440	10,481	10.383	10,235	9,899	8,825	8,977

[1]Organization of Petroleum Exporting Countries.

Source: United States Department of Commerce, Bureau of Economic Analysis, Washington, D.C.

TABLE 25

United States Direct Investment Position Abroad, Selected Pacific Rim Region Members, Yearend 1982-1989
Millions of United States Dollars

	1982	1983	1984	1985	1986	1987	1988	1989
Northwest Quarter								
Japan	6,407	7,661	7,936	9,235	11,472	15,684	17,927	19,341
South Korea	690	589	716	743	782	1,178	1,501	1,889
China, People's Republic	49	100	209	311	167	207	307	370
Taiwan	544	613	736	750	869	1,372	1,,622	1,949
Hong Kong	2,854	3,068	3,253	3,295	3,912	4,389	5,244	5,853
Philippines	1,315	1,331	1,263	1,032	1,299	1,396	1,511	1,682
Vietnam	*	*	*	*	*	*	*	*
Thailand	780	892	1,081	1,074	1,078	1,274	1,132	1,279
Malaysia	1,221	1,157	1,101	1,140	1,021	952	1,135	1,098
Singapore	1,720	1,821	1,932	1,874	2,256	2,384	2,290	2,213
Brunei	D	D	1	*	-29	-18	-18	-20
Southwest Quarter								
Indonesia	2,295	2,770	4,093	4,475	3,217	3,070	2,925	3,696
Papua New Guinea	57	102	147	140	144	151	193	170
Australia	9,089	9,005	8,9118	8,772	9,340	11,363	13,186	14,495
New Zealand	644	566	510	576	598	743	833	1,167
Fiji	D	D	D	D	D	D	D	0
Tonga	D	2	2	2	2	3	3	3
Vanuatu	D	D	D	D	D	D	D	D

TABLE 25 (continued)

United States Direct Investment Position Abroad, Selected Pacific Rim Region Members, Yearend 1982-1989
Millions of United States Dollars

	1982	1983	1984	1985	1986	1987	1988	1989
Southeast Quarter								
Ecuador	388	442	371	361	413	466	431	395
Peru	1,990	2,042	1,902	1,243	1,103	1,022	986	912
Chile	311	108	47	88	265	348	691	1,018
Western Samoa	*	*	*	*	*	*	1	1
French Polynesia	3	2	2	3	3	4	4	4
Northeast Quarter								
Canada	43,511	44,339	46,730	46,909	50,629	57,783	62,610	66,856
Mexico	5,019	4,381	4,597	5,088	4,623	4,913	5,694	7,079
Guatemala	233	214	240	213	181	174	200	221
Honduras	247	216	288	171	167	185	240	318
El Salvador	96	100	94	73	D	51	56	62
Nicaragua	20	35	39	39	51	147	143	143
Costa Rica	142	166	158	113	113	141	169	163
Panama	4,413	4,837	4,474	3,959	5,525	6,622	6,632	7,906
Colombia	1,769	2,123	2,111	2,148	3,291	3,104	2,248	1,900

* Less than $500,000 (+, -)

Source: United States Department of Commerce, Bureau of Economic Analysis, Washington, D.C.

CHAPTER FIVE

An Operational, Practical Approach to the Pacific Rim Region With Respect To Regional Economic and Trade Coordination: The Pacific Rim Region Trade and Economic Organization (PRRTEO)

Before venturing onward with this proposal, please note that the nature of this PRRTEO proposal is concerned with establishing a practical, conceptual framework to openly exchange ideas along with compiling and disseminating trade and economic information. This proposal strongly opposes setting in motion stern conditions for an arduous, institutional format. So whatever details as geographic locations or timetables may seem untenable, they can be changed easily to better suit those involved. As for the practical aspect of the Pacific Rim Region, keep in mind the conceptual nature of the Region, and the profitable advantages it would afford to its diverse membership through the open exchange of ideas along with the exchange of trade and economic information.

In order to coordinate and utilize the Pacific Rim Region concept in a practical fashion, an operational approach for a regional economic and trade organization would prove lucrative for all Region members. PRRTEO membership is voluntary. Any membership among respective Pacific Rim Region members is the prerogative of the economy involved. Those willing to join PRRTEO will profit from the benefits of exchanging timely economic and investment information. The benefits would enhance economic activity and economic growth through basic geographical and economic considerations. With respect to economic considerations, instead of political and/or military alliances, the Pacific Rim Region Trade and Economic Organization would provide an organizational format facilitating peace, trade, direct investment, and understanding. Headquartered in the center of the Region, with various satellite offices among the Region's four Quarters, PRRTEO activities would include:

- to nourish a Pacific Rim Region community atmosphere through a forum for the open exchange of ideas;

- to enhance economic activity and economic growth among member economies through the timely exchange of economic, trade, commercial, and investment activity trends about member economies and the world marketplace;

- to disseminate the above economic, trade, commercial, and investment activity information among the private and public sectors in the Region within a timely fashion, and;

- to consider forming a loose economic association by either coordinating trade and economic policies, instituting preferential tariff treatments, or through trade liberalization programs.

Due to its relative proximity to the center of the Region and its frequent commercial aircraft service, the Hawaiian Islands would serve as a convenient location to host PRRTEO's Home Office. Preferably, the islands of Maui or Kauai would best suit an informal, relaxed atmosphere that enhances productive relationships among participating individuals. Each Region member will participate in biannual Delegaton Conferences occurring at least six months apart in PRRTEO's Home Office facilities.

Each of the Region's forty-six members will be represented by a delegation comprised of at least two private sector individuals and one government representative from either a commerce or foreign affairs department, preferably, a minister of commerce or a minister of foreign affairs. Private sector members would be elected from a National Committee comprised of business people interested in the Region. The National Committee would be open to the general business community in the respective member country. In order to maintain the precarious balance between the private sector's business savvy, and the public sector's national exposure, the National Delegation would include two representatives from the private sector and one representative from the public sector. This National Delegation also would provide an integral communication link between both sectors and would assist with the timely exchange of economic, trade, commercial, and investment information.

Delegation Conferences will include general discussions regarding trade, commercial, and investment activity (tcia) through four self-explanatory, inclusive subject categories: Agriculture, Manufactures, Agriculture/Manufactures, and Services. Corresponding to each subject category, a committee will compile and coordinate pertinent information required to thoroughly evaluate trade, commercial, and investment activity trends within the Region, and in the world marketplace, which affect and/or may affect the Region's economic performance. If deemed necessary, subcommittees may be formed to facilitate the fact finding missions of the four primary committees. All pertinent findings then will be reported during the biannual Delegation Conferences and disseminated promptly to all Region members following each Delegation Conference in the "Bi-Annual Report: Trade, Commercial, and Investment Activity Trends in the Pacific Rim Region."

As for the Agriculture/Manufactures (A/M) and Services categories, A/M includes merchandise goods that tend to cross-over from one category to another; e.g., agricultural machinery, seed production enterprises, and agricultural production facilities that require specialized knowledge in both the agricultural and manufacturing sectors. Those items that are unclassified within the agriculture or manufactures sectors fall within the Services category: banking, finance, real estate, tourism, construction, advertising, etcetera.

Paramount to Delegation Conferences, and the entire PRRTEO concept, is to provide and maintain a forum for an open exchange of ideas. When decision-making events occur, each of the forty-six member economies represent one vote. Only resolutions and recommendations may be voted on. The distinction between a resolution and a recommendation is self-explanatory. Further interpretations may be decided upon by the Delegation Conferences.

Constituting the foundation of PRRTEO encompasses the four Quarters' satellite office system network where a minimum of three satellite offices will operate in each Quarter. Within each Quarter, one satellite office is designated as a Coordinating Agency. The Coordinating Agency compiles and organizes pertinent trade and economic information for their respective Quarter, and shares in the responsibility among their respective Quarter satellite offices to present this information during Delegation Conferences. Satellite Offices and designated Coordinating Agencies are:

TABLE 26

PRRTEO's Satellite Offices and Designated Coordinating Agencies

Northwest Quarter (NWQ)
- Tokyo, Japan
- Beijing, China
- Bangkok, Thailand - NWQ Coordinating Agency

Southwest Quarter (SWQ)
- Jakarta, Indonesia
- Sydney, Australia
- Auckland, New Zealand - SWQ Coordinating Agency

Southeast Quarter (SEQ)
- Quito, Ecuador - SEQ Coordinating Agency
- Santiago, Chile
- Papeete, Tahiti

Northeast Quarter (NEQ)
- Vancouver, Canada - NEQ Coordinating Agency
- Seattle, Washington
- San Jose, Costa Rica

Perhaps one satellite office per Region member would produce more accurate and insightful information than relying on three offices to act as information conduits for an entire Quarter. Whatever the choice, until adequate funding is available, satellite offices may consider locating adjacent to chamber of commerce-oriented operations in their respective markets. Similar to Delegation Conferences, satellite offices within each Quarter will meet biannually as well. However, biannual satellite meetings must occur prior to Delegation Conferences to ensure timely and accurate evaluations for each Quarter's trade, commercial, and investment activity.

In order to avoid any misunderstandings about this PRRTEO proposal, PRRTEO simply operationalizes the Pacific Rim Region concept and the profitable advantages it would afford to its diverse membership through the open exchange of ideas along with the exchange of trade and economic information. When considering PRRTEO's one-member one-vote method, it is similar to the current United Nations General Assembly voting system. Quintessentially, this proposal strongly opposes setting in motion stern conditions for an arduous, institutional format. Rather, PRRTEO provides a conceptual framework that operationalizes the Pacific Rim Region's association. Whatever details as geographic locations, timetables, statistical techniques, streamlined methods, publications, and the like; may seem untenable, they can be changed easily to better suit those involved. For the primary objective of PRRTEO is to operationalize the Pacific Rim Region in order to profitably benefit its members through the open exchange of ideas, along with the exchange of trade and economic information.

CHAPTER SIX

Concluding Comments

Utilizing geographical and economic considerations, this book inclusively defines and quantifies the contemporary Pacific Rim Region concept. Given that trans-Pacific trade activity continues to burgeon beyond trans-Atlantic trade, since the early 1980s, the Pacific Rim Region concept presented here provides a practical and operational analytical tool for the private and public sectors. Transcending political and military overtones, geoeconomics acknowledges the Pacific Rim Region area as the *common* geographical feature linking a diverse membership together. Awash with numerous cultural differences within the Region, and the world, a common thread links many people. That thread is economic prosperity. Although each market may pursue different paths, all economies strive toward the common objective of economic prosperity in terms of cultural beliefs and national values. Acknowledging this quest toward economic prosperity, our relationship to the land, and efficiently cultivating the natural resources that it offers, geoeconomics utilizes these fundamental basics for evaluating the immense Pacific Rim Region.

In today's world of integrated markets, rising bilateralism, coordinated market efforts, and expanding protectionism, the Pacific Rim Region plays an integral part in the rapidly deteriorating post-World Wars, bipolar international nation-state era. As we effectively utilize and enhance new technologies from worldwide instant voice communications, immediate capital transfers, facsimile transmissions, to enlarged and more efficient aircraft and containerized shipping transportation facilities, we find ourselves at the threshold of a genuine Global Economic Market Epoch. From global communications to transportation, the world is perceived as a more accessible, diversified marketplace for suppliers and consumers instead of an arena for the few transnational corporations.

Economically, the current hegemonic nature of the global market, in terms of production and consumption, gravitates about the European Communities (particularly West Germany), Japan, and the United States. Within these spheres of regional and global economic influences, a trade and economic organization, the Pacific Rim Region

Trade and Economic Organization embodies and operationalizes the Pacific Rim Region concept. Dedicated to peace, trade, direct investment, and understanding, PRRTEO auspiciously espouses a forum for the open exchange of ideas, and to provide for the exchange of trade and economic information in order to enhance trade and investment activities within the Region. Even if favorable tariff rates and coordinated trade policies prove unmanageable through PRRTEO, that is fine; because paramount to a diversified, forty-six member multilateral organization is to pursue and *maintain* the open exchange of information and ideas. As long as avenues of communication remain open, an expanding awareness of the members will evolve, which will eventually foster enhanced trade and investment activities throughout the Region. For through understanding, the benefits are immense and, at times, difficult to quantify.

In time, the Pacific Rim Region, the European Communities, and other coordinated market efforts one day will be considered provincial and limited with respect to the entire global community. Minus political overtones and hostilities, which tend to arise among different economic philosophies, perhaps a global, economic-cooperative organizational vision would emerge dedicated to genuine peace, trade, and understanding. Such a moment in human history would truly mark forceful change in the human condition. Until all members of the global community earnestly focus on *common* goals — in this sense, geoeconomic goals — regional trade organizations will simply suffice.

NOTES

[1]Colombo Plan Members: Afghanistan, Australia, Bangladesh, Bhutan, Burma, Canada, Fiji, India, Indonesia, Iran, Japan, Kampuchea, Republic of Korea, Lao People's Democratic Republic, Malaysia, Maldives, Nepal, New Zealand, Pakistan, Papua New Guinea, Philippines, Singapore, Sri Lanka, Thailand, UK and USA.

[2]Colombo Plan, EC, EFTA, and ASEAN information was primarily obtained from: John Paxton, *The Statesman's Yearbook 1990-91*, 127th ed. (New York: St. Martin's Press, 1990), 42-52.

[3]Laroslav Vanek, *International Trade: Theory and Economic Policy* (Homewood, Illinois: Richard D. Irwin, Incorporated, 1962), 345-47.

[4]Susumu Aklanohara, "Brave New World: Latin American revival could give Asia a run for its money," *Far Eastern Economic Review*, 13 September 1990, Vol. 149, No. 37, 48-9.

[5]Congressional Research Service, Library of Congress, *An Asian-Pacific Regional Economic Organization: An Explanatory Concept Paper*, prepared for the Committee on Foreign Relations, United States Senate (Washington, D.C.: U.S. Government Printing Office, 1979).

[6]R. Sean Randolph, "Pacific Overtures," *Foreign Policy*, Number 57, Winter 1984-5, 129-130.

[7]*Ibid.*, 130.

Congressional Research Service, Library of Congress, *An Asian-Pacific Regional Economic Organization: An Explanatory Concept Paper*, prepared for the Committee on Foreign Relations, United States Senate (Washington, D.C.: U.S. Government Printing Office, 1979).

[9]"Pacific Rim Nations Unlikely To Form Block," *Journal of Commerce and Commercial*, 8 May 1990, Vol. 384, 4A(1).

[10]"Puffery In the Pacific," *The Economist*, 11 November 1989, Vol. 313, 14(1).

[11]Carl Goldstein, "Unstitching the Pact," *Far Eastern Economic Review*, 16 August 1990, Vol. 149, No. 33, 56-7.

[12]*Far Eastern Economic Review*, 22 November 1990, Vol. 150, No. 47, 74-5.

[13]International Monetary Fund, *World Economic Outlook, A Survey by the Staff of the International Monetary Fund*, Washington, D.C., May 1990 (edition).

[14]"America's Debt Burden Soars to $535 Billion," *International Herald Tribune*, 30 June 1989.

[15]Organization for Economic Cooperation and Development, *Geographical Distribution of Financial Flows*, (1988 edition only).

[16]*Ibid.*

[17]"Puffery In the Pacific," *The Economist*, 11 November 1989, Vol. 313, 14(1).

[18]Aspects of trade policy and Maekawa Report derived from: The Tsuneta Yano Memorial Society (Yano-Tsuneta Kinenkai), ed., *Nippon, A Charted Survey of Japan 1988/89* (Tokyo, Japan: The Kokusei-sha Corporation, August 1988); and United States Department of Commerce, International Trade Administration, "Japan: Foreign Economic Trends and Their Implications for the United States" (Washington, D.C.: October 1988).

[19]International Monetary Fund, *Exchange Arrangements and Exchange Restrictions Annual Report 1988*, Washington, D.C., 261.

[20]*Ibid.*

[21]*Ibid.*

[22]*Ibid.*

[23]*Ibid.*, 262.

[24]*Ibid.*

[25]*Ibid.*

[26]*Ibid.*

[27]*Ibid.*, 263.

[28]James Sterngold, "Japanese Capitalize on Rising Tokyo Market," *International Herald Tribune*, 28-29 October 1989.

[29]Susuma Awanohara, "The Rising Sun: Tokyo's trade surplus and acquisitions fuel American backlash," *Far Eastern Economic Review*, 8 February 1990, Vol. 147, No. 6, 24-7.

[30]*Ibid.*

[31] Space program's facts, figures, and comparisons are compiled primarily from two sources: David E. Sanger, "Japan Strives for the Ultimate Horizon: Business in Space," *International Herald Tribune*, 12-13 May 1990, and "Greatest Little Space Agency In The Universe (Japan's Insitute of Space and Astronomical Science)," *Asia Technology*, August 1990, 50-5.

[32]General Agreement of Tariffs and Trade, *Trade Policy Review, Australia 1989* (Geneva: March 1990), 82.

[33]Ian Castles, *Yearbook Australia 1989*, No. 72, (Canberra: Australian Bureau of Statistics, 1989), 764.

[34]General Agreement of Tariffs and Trade, *Trade Policy Review, Australia 1989* (Geneva: March 1990), 30.

[35]*Ibid.*, 31.

[36]International Monetary Fund, *Exchange Arrangements and Exchange Restrictions Annual Report 1988*, Washington, D.C., 19.

[37]*Ibid.*

[38]*Ibid.*

[39]*Ibid.*, 20-1.

[40]*Ibid.*, 21.

[41]*Ibid.*, 22.

[42]*Ibid.*

[43]General Agreement of Tariffs and Trade, *Trade Policy Review, Australia 1989* (Geneva: March 1990), 103-4.

[44]*Ibid.*, 104.

[45]Michael Richardson, "In Australia, Setbacks for a 'SuperCity'," *International Herald Tribune*, 4 April 1990, 8(2).

[46]Ian Castles, *Yearbook Australia 1989*, No. 72 (Canberra: Australian Bureau of Statistics, 1989), 48.

[47]Inter-American Development Bank, *Economic and Social Progress in Latin America*, Annual Report: 1989, 25.

[48]United States Department of Commerce, International Trade Administration, "Chile: Foreign Economic Trends and Their Implications for the United States," (Washington D.C.: January 1990).

[49]World of Information, *The Latin America and Caribbean Review* (Essex, United Kingdom: NTC Business Books, A Division of NTC Publishing Group, 1989), 51.

[50]United States Department of Commerce, International Trade Administration, "Chile: Foreign Economic Trends and Their Implications for the United States," (Washington, D.C.: January 1990), 4.

[51]International Monetary Fund, *Exchange Arrangements and Exchange Restrictions Annual Report 1988*, Washington, D.C., 96.

[52]*Ibid.*, 96-7.

[53]*Ibid.*, 96.

[54]*Ibid.*, 97.

[55]*Ibid.*

[56]*Ibid.*

[57]*Ibid.*, 98.

[58]*Ibid.*

[59]*Ibid.*

[60]World of Information, *The Latin America and Caribbean Review* (Essex, United Kingdom: NTC Business Books, A Division of NTC Publishing Group, 1989), 48-9.

[61]Economist Intelligence Unit, *Country Profile, Chile* (London, England: The Economist Intelligence Unit, 1988), 19.

[62]*Omnibus Trade and Competitiveness Act of 1988, U.S. Code*, Vol. 19, Sec. 2901 (1988).

[63]OECD, *OECD Economic Surveys, United States* (Paris, France, 1989), 128.

[64]*Ibid.*, 101-2.

[65]Jacob M. Schlesinger, "U.S., Japan Set Pact They See Easing Tension," *The Wall Street Journal*, 29 June 1990.

[66]Richard Lawrence, "Bush Proposes Trade Zone for Western Hemisphere," *Journal of Commerce and Commercial*, 8 May 1990, Vol. 384, 4A(1).

[67] Western Hemisphere free-trade initiative specifics derived primarily from two sources: Richard Lawrence, "Bush Proposes Trade Zone for Western Hemisphere," *Journal of Commerce and Commercial*, 8 May 1990, Vol. 384, 4A(1); and Peter Truell and Michel McQueen, "Bush Acts to Aid Latin America On Debt, Trade," *The Wall Street Journal*, 28 June 1990, 34.

[68]Office of the Federal Register, National Archives and Records Administration, *The United States Government Manual 1989-1990* (Washington, D.C.: U.S. Government Printing Office, July 1989), 563.

[69]*Ibid*., 562-4.

[70]International Monetary Fund, *Exchange Arrangements and Exchange Restrictions Annual Report 1988*, Washington, D.C., 514.

[71]International Monetary Fund, *Exchange Arrangements and Exchange Restrictions Annual Report 1988*, Washington, D.C., 514. GSP members include: Bangladesh, Benin, Bhutan, Botswana, Burkina Faso, Burundi, Cape Verde, Central African Republic, Chad, Comoros, Djibouti, Equatorial Guinea, The Gambia, Guinea, Guinea-Bissau, Haiti, Lesotho, Malawi, Maldives, Mali, Nepal, Niger, Rwanda, Sao Tome and Principe, Sierra Leone, Somalia, Sudan, Tanzania, Togo, Uganda, Western Samoa, and Yemen Arab Republic.

[72]*Ibid*., 516.

[73]*Ibid*., 516.

[74]Emily Smith, "Glimpsing the Future in the Number," *Business Week*, Innovation 1990, A Special Issue, 195.

[75]Organization for Economic Cooperation and Development, *Geographical Distribution of Financial Flows* (Paris, France: 1985/1988).

[76]Barclays Economic Department, "Country Report, United States" (London, England: Barclays Bank PLC, March 1990).

[77]*Ibid.*

[78]*Ibid.*, 3.

[79]John W. Wright, *The Universal Almanac* (Kansas City and New York: Andrews and McMeel, 1989), 295.

[80]Leonard Silk, "U.S. Is Exporting Factories, Not Goods, Trend Makes Deficit Cuts Harder," *International Herald Tribune*, 2-3 June 1990.

BIBLIOGRAPHY

"Pacific Tale." *The Economist*, November 1988, Vol. 13, 39 (1).

"A Strategic Guide to the Rim." Special Issue. *Fortune*, Autumn 1989, Volume 120, 72 (8).

"A Survey of the European Community." *The Economist*, 7-13 July 1990, Vol. 316, No. 7662, 53.

Aikman, David. *Pacific Rim: Area of Change, Area of Opportunity*. Boston and Toronto: Little, Brown and Company, 1987.

"America's Debt Burden Soars to $535 Billion." *International Herald Tribune*, 30 June 1989.

Awanohara, Susuma. "Brave New World: Latin American revival could give Asia a run for its money." *Far Eastern Economic Review*, 13 September 1990, Vol. 149, No. 37, 48-9.

Awanohara, Susuma. "The New Economic Order: Japan secures equal second place in IMF." *Far Eastern Economic Review*, 17 May 1990, Vol. 148, No. 20, 72-3.

Awanohara, Susuma. "The Rising Sun: Tokyo's trade surplus and acquisitions fuel American backlash." *Far Eastern Economic Review*, 8 February 1990, Vol. 147, No. 6, 24-7.

Barclays Economic Department, "Country Report, United States." London, England: Barclays Bank PLC, March 1990.

Belous, Richard S. and Hartley, Rebecca S., eds. *The Growth of Regional Trading Blocs in the Global Economy*. Washington, D.C.: National Planning Association, 1990.

Belsham, Cyril. *Changing Melanesia, Social Economics of Cultural Contact*. Melborne and Wellington: Oxford University Press, 1954.

Belton, Beth. "Japan's No. 1 Refocuses Global Vision." *USA Today*, 24 May 1990.

Black, Jan Knippers, ed. *Latin America, Its Problems and Its Promise*. Boulder and London: Western Press, 1984.

Banovia, David. *The Chinese*. Hermondsworth, Middlesex, England: Penguin Books Limited, 1982.

Brauchli, Marcus W. "Attitudes Change on Japan's Shareholders." *The Wall Street Journal*, 27 June 1989, 10A(2).

Brookfield, H.S. *Colonialism, Development and Independence, The Case of the Melanesian Island in the South Pacific*. Cambridge: The University Press, 1972.

Bunge, Fredrick and Cooke, Melinda, eds. *Oceania: A Regional Study*. Washington, D.C.: Department of the Army, June 1984.

Cassen, Robert and Associates. *Does Aid Work? Report to an Intergovernmental Task Force*. Oxford: Clarendon Press, 1986.

Castles, Ian. *Yearbook Australia 1989*, No. 72. Canberra: Australian Bureau of Statistics, 1989.

Chaliand, Gérard and Pageau, Jean-Pierre. *A Strategic Atlas, Comparative Geopolitics of the World's Powers*. Second Edition. New York and Sydney: Harper & Row, Publishers, Incorporated, 1985.

Congressional Research Service, Library of Congress. *An Asian-Pacific Regional Economic Organization: An Explanatory Concept Paper*, prepared for the Committee on Foreign Relations, United States Senate. Washington, D.C.: U.S. Government Printing Office, 1979.

Cussans, Lisa and Farndon, John, eds. *The Economist Business Traveller's Guide: United States*. New York, N.Y.: Prentice Hall, 1987.

"Democracy Returns To Chile After 16 Years As Pinochet Bows Out." *International Herald Tribune*, 12 March 1990, 4.

Department of Resources and Development. *Federated States of Micronesia Investment Guide*. Kolonia, Pohnpei: Federated States of Micronesia National Government, August 1988.

Dowen, Robert and Dickson, Bruce, Editors. *The Emerging Pacific Community: A Regional Perspective*. Boulder, Colorado: Westview Press, 1984.

Economist Intelligence Unit. *Country Profile, Chile*. London, England: The Economist Intelligence Unit, 1988.

Edwards, Sebasian and Edwards, Alejandra Cox. *Monetarism and Liberalization, The Chilean Experiment*. Cambridge, Massachusetts: Ballinger Publishing Company, 1987.

Erlanger, Steven. "Economic Rivalries Fuel Asian Rivalries." *International Herald Tribune*, 7 May 1990.

Esselle Map Service. *The Concise Earthbook*. Boulder, Colorado: Graphic Learning International Publishing Corporation, 1987.

Fairbanks, John K. *The United States and China*. 4th ed. Cambridge, Massachusetts: Harvard University, 1974.

Far Eastern Economic Review. *Asia 1989 Yearbook*. Hong Kong: Review Publishing Limited, 1989.

Far Eastern Economic Review. *Asia 1990 Yearbook*. Hong Kong: Review Publishing Limited, 1990.

Fitchett, Joseph. "At NATO Meeting, Japan Seeks Wider Security Link." *International Herald Tribune*, 20 June 1990, 1(2).

Galuszka, Peter, ed. "Is A Grand Alliance In The Making On The Pacific Rim." *Business Week*, 6 November 1984, 70(1).

"GATT and Intellectual Property, Thought Control." *The Economist*, 7-13 July 1990, Vol. 316, No. 7662, 68.

General Agreement on Tariffs and Trade. *Trade Policy Review, Australia 1989*. Geneva: March 1990.

Gewirtz, Carl. "Bank Overseers Aim to Broaden Regulations." *International Herald Tribune*, 6 June 1990.

Gewirtz, Carl. "Market Woes, Restricted to Tokyo, Fail to Stir G-7." *International Herald Tribune*, 3 April 1990.

Goldstein, Carl. "Blown By The Trade Winds." *Far Eastern Economic Review*, 16 August 1990, Vol. 149, No. 33, 54-57.

Goldstein, Carl. "Unstitching the Pact." *Far Eastern Economic Review*, 16 August 1990, Vol. 149, No. 33, 56-57.

"Greatest Little Space Agency In The Universe (Japan's Institute of Space and Astronomical Science)." *Asia Technology*, August 1990, 50-55.

Harding, Harry: *China's Second Revolution*. Washington, D.C.: The Brookings Institution, 1987.

Harrison, Selig S. and Prestowitz, Clyde V., Jr. "Pacific Agenda: Defense in Economics?" *Foreign Policy*, No. 79, Summer 1990, 56-76.

Hayter, Teresa and Watson, Catherine. *Aid: Rhetoric or Reality*. London: Pluto Press, 1985.

Hiatt, Fred. "A Japanese Dilemma: How to Spend All That Yen." *International Herald Tribune*, 12 February 1990.

Hiatt, Fred. "Japan: Is the Sun Setting on an Era of Economic Expansion." *International Herald Tribune*, 16-17 September 1989, No. 33, 145.

Hillkirk, John. "Japanese Renew Efforts To Find U.S. Oil." *USA Today*, 25 June 1990, 2.

Hoffman, Mark S., ed. *The World Almanac and Book of Facts*. New York, N.Y.: Pharos Books, 1990.

Inter-American Development Bank. *Economic and Social Progress in Latin America*, Various Annual Reports: 1989, 1988, 1987, and 1983. Washington, D.C.

International Bank for Reconstruction and Development. *World Development Report*. Two Editions 1988 and 1989. Washington, D.C.

International Monetary Fund. *Direction of Trade Statistics*, Various Editions: 1989, 1988, and 1984. Washington, D.C.

International Monetary Fund. *Exchange Arrangements and Exchange Restrictions Annual Report 1988*. Washington, D.C.

International Monetary Fund. *Exchange Arrangements and Exchange Restrictions Annual Report 1989*. Washington, D.C.

International Monetary Fund. *International Financial Statistics Yearbook*. Two Editions 1989 and 1988. Washington, D.C.

International Monetary Fund. *World Economic Outlook, A Survey by the Staff of the International Monetary Fund*. Washington, D. C., October 1989 and May 1990.

"Japan Aids Mexico on Smog." *International Herald Tribune*, 20 August 1990.

"Japan Cautions Firms on Buying spree Overseas." *International Herald Tribune*, 31 January 1990.

"Japan Reconsiders Role of Trade Surplus." *International Herald Tribune*, 2-3 June 1990.

"Japan's New Gospel, Kaifu signals Tokyo's desire for influence in Asia." *Far Eastern Economic Review*, 17 May 1990, Vol. 148, No. 20, 13.

Jeffries, Brian. "Japan Launches A Rocket Firm" *Asia Technology*, July 1990, 37.

Kim, Roy and Conroy, Hilary, eds. *New Tides in the Pacific: Pacific Basin Cooperation and the Big Four (Japan, PRC, USA, USSR)*. New York and London: Greewood Press, 1987.

Kristof, Nicholas D. "Beneath China's Still Surface, 'Explosive' Instability Seethes, An Ancient Could Repeat Itself." *International Herald Tribune*, 16 April 1990, No. 33, 323.

Lawerence, Richard. "Bush Proposes Trade Zone For Western Hemisphere." *Journal of Commerce and Commercial*, 8 May 1990, Vol. 384, 4A(1).

Lawerence, Anthony. *China: The Long March*. London: Merehurst Press, 1986.

Maniketh, Vijayan. "Scaled-Down Silicon Valley (in Bangalore, India)." *Asia Technology*, July 1990. 45-47.

Morse, Ronald A., Editor. *Pacific Basin; Concept and Challenge*. Washington, D.C. : Center for National Policy, 1986.

Mosley, Paul. *Foreign Aid: Its Defense and Reform*. Lexington: The University Press of Kentucky, 1987.

Nemetz, Peter N., Editor. *The Pacific Rim: Investment, Development, and Trade*. Vancouver, B.C.: University of British Columbia Press, 1987.

Oborne, Michael West and Fourt, Nicolas. *Pacific Basin Economic Cooperation*. Paris: Development Centre of the OECD, 1983.

"OECD Aid To Poor Countries Drops." *International Herald Tribune*, 25 June 1990.

Office of Planning and Statistics. *Investment Guide to the Republic of Palau (Belau)*. Koror, Republic of Palau: 1985.

Office of Planning and Statistics. *Marshall Islands Investment Guide*. Majuro, Marshall Islands: 1989.

Office of the Federal Register, National Archives and Records Administration. *The United States Government Manual 1989-1990*. Washington, D.C.: U.S. Government Printing Office, July 1989.

Omnibus Trade and Competitiveness Act of 1988. *United States Code*, Vol. 19, Sec. 2901 (1988).

Organization for Economic Cooperation and Development. *Geographical Distribution of Financial Flows*. Numerous Yearbooks: 1979/1982, 1984/1986, 1985/1988. Paris, France.

Organization for Economic Cooperation and Development. *OECD Economic Surveys, United States*. Paris, France. 1989.

Pacific Basin Economic Council. *PEC, Pacific Economic Community Statistics 1986*. Japan; PBEC Japan Member Committee, 1986.

"Pacific Rim Nations Unlikely To Form Block." *Journal of Commerce and Commercial*, 8 May 1990, Vol. 384, 4A(1).

Paxton, John, ed. *The Statesman's Yearbook 1990-91.* 27th Ed. New York: St. Martin's Press, 1990.

Phillips, Douglas A. and Levi, Steven C. *The Pacific Rim Region: Emerging Giant.* Hillside, New Jersey: Enslow Publishers, Incorporated, 1988.

"Puffery In The Pacific." *The Economist*, 11 November 1989, Vol. 313, 14(1).

Pye, Lucian W. "On Chinese Pragmatism in the 1980s." The China Quarterly, No. 106, June 1986, 207-34.

Randolph, R. Sean "Pacific Overtures," *Foreign Policy*, Number 57, Winter 1984-5, 128-142.

Republic of Palau. "Business Associations, Title 12." Koror, Palau: 1989.

Republic of Palau. "Foreign Relations and Trade, Title 28." Koror, Palau: 1989.

Richardson, Michael. "In Australia, Setbacks for a 'SuperCity'." *International Herald Tribune*, 4 April 1990, 8(2).

Sanger, David E. "Japan Strives for the Ultimate Horizon: Business in Space." *International Herald Tribune*, 12-13 May 1990.

Sanger, David E. "Vacuum in Hong Kong Draws in the Japanese." *International Herald Tribune*, 30 May 1990.

Schell, Orville. *To Get Rich is Glorious.* New York, New York: Pantheon Books, 1984.

Schlesinger, Jacob M. "U.S., Japan Set Pact They See Easing Tension." *The Wall Street Journal*, 29 June 1990.

Shapiro, Margaret. "An Anxious World Watches as Japan Pursues a New Destiny." *International Herald Tribune*, 24 February 1990.

Shand, R. T. and Richter, H. V., eds. *International AID: Some Political, Administrative and Technical Realities*. Canberra: The Australian National University, 1979.

Silk, Leonard. "U.S. Is Exporting Factories, Not Goods, Trend Makes Deficit Cuts Harder." *International Herald Tribune*, 2-3 June 1990.

Sinclair, Keith. *A History of New Zealand*. Middlesex, England: Penguin Books Limited, 1980.

Smith, Emily. "Glimpsing the Future in the Number." *Business Week*, Innovation 1990, A Special Issue, 194-196.

Smith, Patrick L. "Japan in East Asia: A Boom Pays Off, Decade of Investment Creates Bloc, Leaving US and Europe Behind." *International Herald Tribune*, 30 May 1990.

Smith, Charles. "No Interest in Japan: Capital Outflow Triggers Rate Increase." *Far Eastern Economic Review*, 11 January 1990, Vol. 147, No. 2, 36-37.

Smith, Patrick. "Tokyo's OTC Comes of Age, New funds hope to profit from enthusiasm." *International Herald Tribune*, 12 February 1990.

Sterngold, James. "A Question in Japan on Aid for Eastern Europe: What's in it for us?" *International Herald Tribune*, 27-28 January 1990.

Sterngold, James. "Japan Puts Off Its Favorite Son in Peru." *International Herald Tribune*, 13 June 1990.

Sterngold, James. "Japanese Capitalize on Rising Tokyo Market." *International Herald Tribune*, 28-29 October 1989.

Stillwell, Rodger. Editor. *Micronesian Investment Quarterly*, Summer 1989, 1st Quarter 1990, 2nd Quarter 1990; Vol. 1; Issues 1, 2, 3.

Swift, Jeannie. *Economic Development in Latin America*. New York, N.Y. : Saint Martin's Press, Incorporated, 1978.

"Taiwan Blasts Japan on Trade." *International Herald Tribune*, 16-17 June 1990.

Taylor, Michael. "Business Knows Best." *Far Eastern Economic Review*, 8 March 1990, Vol. 147, No. 10, 41(1).

"The New Powers of Asia." *Fortune*, 28 March 1988, Vol. 117, 126(7).

The Tsuneta Yano Memorial Society (Yano-Tsuneta Kinenkai), ed. *Nippon, A Charted Survey of Japan 1988/89*. Tokyo, Japan: The Kokusei-sha Corporation, August 1988.

"The Yen Block Survey." *The Economist*, 11 November 1989, Vol. 313, 39(1).

Truell, Peter and McQueen, Michel. "Bush Acts to Aid Latin America On Debt, Trade." *The Wall Street Journal*, 28 June 1990, 34.

Uchitelle, Louis. "U.S. Is Exporting Factories, Not Goods, Trend Makes Deficit Cuts Harder." *International Herald Tribune*, 3 April 1990.

United Nations. *International Trade Statistics Yearbook*. Various Issues 1984, 1985, 1988. New York, N.Y.

United Nations. United Nations Centre on Transnational Corporations. *Transnational Corporations in World Development, Trends and Prospects*. New York and Geneva: 1988.

United Nations. Department of International and Social Affairs. *World Economic Survey 1989, Current Trends and Policies in the World Economy*. New York: 1984.

United Nations. Department of International Economic and Social Affairs. *World Economic Survey 1990, Current Trends and Policies in the World Economy*. New York: 1990.

United States Department of Commerce, Bureau of the Census. *Statistical Abstract of the United States 1990*. Washington, D.C.: U.S. Government Printing Office, 1990.

United States Department of Commerce. International Trade Administration. "Australia: Foreign Economic Trends and Their Implications for the United States." Washington, D. C. : September 1989.

United States Department of Commerce. International Trade Administration. "Chile: Foreign Economic Trends and Their Implications for the United States." Washington, D.C. : January 1990.

United States Department of Commerce. International Trade Administration. *International Direct Investment: Global Trends and the U.S. Role*. Washington, D.C. : Two Editions: August 1984 and November 1988.

United States Department of Commerce. International Trade Administration. "Japan: Foreign Economic Trends and Their Implications for the United States." Washington, D.C. : October 1988.

United States Department of State. Bureau of Public Affairs, Background Notes. "Australia." Washington, D.C. : March 1989.

United States Department of State. Bureau of Public Affairs, Background Notes. "Chile." Washington, D.C. : September 1988.

United States Department of State. Bureau of Public Affairs, Background Notes. "Japan." Washington, D.C. : February 1989.

Van Horn, Mike. *Pacific Rim Trade: The Definitive Guide to Exporting and Investment*. New York: AMACON, 1989.

Vanek, Laroslav. *International Trade: Theory and Economic Policy*. Homewood, Illinois: Richard D. Irwin, Incorporated, 1962.

Ward, J.R. *Poverty and Progress in the Caribbean 1800-1960*. London. Macmillan Publishers Limited, 1985.

Ward, R. Gerald. Editor. *Man in the Pacific Islands*. Oxford: Clarendon Press, 1969.

Weisman, Steven R. "As Japan Comes of Age, U.S. Rethinks Partnership." *International Herald Tribune*, 5 June 1990.

West, Philip, Editor. *The Pacific Rim and the Western World: Strategic, Economic, and Cultural Perspectives*. Boulder, Colorado: Westview Press, 1987.

Wilke, James W. and Ochoa, Enrique, eds. *Statistical Abstract of Latin America, Volume 27*. Los Angeles: UCLA Latin American Center Publications, 1988.

World of Information. *The Asia and Pacific Review*. Essex, United Kingdom: NTC Business Books, a Division of NTC Publishing Group, 1989.

World of Information. *The Latin America and Caribbean Review*. Essex, United Kingdom: NTC Business Books, A Division of NTC Publishing Group, 1989.

Wright, John W. *The Universal Almanac*. Kansas City and New York: Andrews and McMeel, 1989.

APPENDIX

Major Export and Import Partners of Pacific Rim Region Members For 1978 and 1988.

APPENDIX

Major Export and Import Partners of Pacific Rim Region Members For 1978 and 1988

	1978	1988
Northwest Quarter		
Japan		
Export partners:	US, FRG, South Korea	US, FRG, South Korea, Taiwan
Import partners:	US, Saudi Arabia, Indonesia, UAE	US, South Korea, Australia, Taiwan, USSR
Soviet Union		
Export partners:	GDR, Poland, Bulgaria, Czechoslovakia	GDR, Poland, Bulgaria, Czechoslovakia
Import partners:	GDR, Poland, Czechoslovakia, Bulgaria	GDR, Poland, Bulgaria, Czechoslovakia
North Korea		
Export partners:	USSR, Saudi Arabia, GDR, FRG	USSR, PRC, Japan, FRG, Hong Kong
Import partners:	USSR, PRC, Japan, India	USSR, PRC, Japan, FRG, Hong Kong
South Korea		
Export partners:	US, Japan, FRG, Saudi Arabia	US, Japan, Hong Kong, FRG
Import partners:	Japan, US, Saudi Arabia, Kuwait	Japan, US, FRG, Australia, Malaysia
China		
Export partners:	Hong Kong, Japan, US, FRG	Hong Kong, Japan, US, FRG
Import partners:	Japan, US, Hong Kong, FRG	Hong Kong, Japan, US, FRG, Singapore
Taiwan		
Export partners:	US, Japan, Hong Kong, FRG	US, Japan, Hong Kong
Import partners:	Japan, US, Kuwait, Saudi Arabia	Japan, US, Saudi Arabia

APPENDIX (continued)
Major Export and Import Partners of Pacific Rim Region Members For 1978 and 1988

	1978	1988
Hong Kong		
Export partners:	US, FRG, UK, China	US, China, FRG, UK, Japan
Import partners:	Japan, China, US, Singapore	China, Japan, Taiwan, US
Philippines		
Export partners:	US, Japan, Netherlands, FRG	US, Japan, Singapore, Hong Kong, UK
Import partners:	US, Japan, Saudi Arabia, Kuwait	US, Japan, Taiwan, Hong Kong, Saudi Arabia
Laos		
Export partners:	Japan, Thailand, US, Singapore	Thailand, Malaysia, Vietnam, USSR, US
Import partners:	Thailand, Japan, Singapore, Sweden	Thailand, USSR, Japan, France, Vietnam Vietnam
Vietnam		
Export partners:	USSR, Japan, Singapore, Hong Kong	USSR, Eastern Europe, Japan, Singapore
Import partners:	USSR, France, FRG, Japan	USSR, Eastern Europe, Japan, Singapore
Kampuchea		
Export partners:	China, N. Korea, Hong Kong, Japan	Vietnam, USSR, Eastern Europe, Japan, India
Import partners:	China, N. Korea, Hong Kong, Japan	Vietnam, USSR, Eastern Europe, Japan, India
Thailand		
Export partners:	Japan, Netherlands, US, Singapore	US, Japan, Singapore, Netherlands, Malaysia
Import partners:	Japan, US, Saudi Arabia, Singapore	Japan, US, Singapore, FRG, Malaysia
Myanmar		
Export partners:	Switzerland, Singapore, Hong Kong, Sri Lanka	US, Japan, EC, India, Africa
Import partners:	Japan, US, UK, FRG	US, Japan, EC China, Thailand
Malaysia		
Export partners:	Japan, Singapore, US, Netherlands	Japan, US, Singapore, Netherlands
Import partners:	Japan, US, Singapore Saudi Arabia	Japan, US, Singapore

APPENDIX (continued)

Major Export and Import Partners of Pacific Rim Region Members For 1978 and 1988

		1978	1988
Singapore			
	Export partners:	Malaysia, US, Japan, Hong Kong	US, Malaysia, Japan, Hong Kong
	Import partners:	Japan, US, Malaysia, Saudi Arabia	Japan, US, Malaysia, Saudi Arabia
Brunei			
	Export partners:	Japan, US, Singapore	Japan, Singapore, Thailand, US
	Import partners:	Japan, Singapore, US, UK	Singapore, US, Japan, UK
Micronesia			
	Export partners:	US, Japan, Guam	US, Japan, Guam
	Import partners:	US, Japan	US, Japan
Marshall Islands			
	Export partners:	US, Japan, Guam	US, Japan, Guam
	Import partners:	US, Japan	US, Japan
Palau			
	Export partners:	US, Japan, Guam	US, Japan, Guam
	Import partners:	US, Japan	US, Japan
Southwest Quarter			
Australia			
	Export partners:	Japan, US, USSR, UK	Japan, US, New Zealand, S. Korea
	Import partners	US, Japan, UK, FRG	US, Japan, UK, FRG
Indonesia			
	Export partners:	Japan, US, Singapore	Japan, US, Singapore, EC
	Import partners:	Japan, US, Saudi Arabia, Singapore	Japan, US, EC, Singapore
Papau New Guinea			
	Export partners:	Japan, FRG, Australia, UK	Japan, FRG, Australia, UK, Spain, US
	Import partners:	Australia, Japan, Singapore	Australia, Japan, Singapore, US, New Zealand

APPENDIX (continued)

Major Export and Import Partners of Pacific Rim Region Members For 1978 and 1988

	1978	1988
New Zealand		
Export partners:	US, UK, Australia, Japan	Japan, US, Australia, UK
Import partners:	Australia, Japan, US, UK	Japan, Australia, US, UK
Solomon Islands		
Export partners:	Japan, UK, Netherlands, American Samoa	Japan, UK, Thailand, Netherlands
Import partners:	Australia, Japan, Singapore, UK	Japan, US, Singapore, UK
Fiji		
Export partners:	UK, New Zealand, US, Malaysia	UK, Australia, US
Import partners:	Australia, New Zealand, Japan, Singapore	New Zealand, Australia, Japan, US
New Caledonia		
Export partners	y --	France, Japan, US, French Polynesia
Import partners	--	France, Australia, Other EC, US
Tonga		
Export partners:	Netherlands, FRG, New Zealand, UK	New Zealand, Australia, US, Fiji
Import partners:	New Zealand, Australia, Japan, Fiji	New Zealand, Australia, Japan US
Tuvalu		
Export partners:	Australia, New Zealand	Fiji, Australia, New Zealand
Import partners:	Australia, New Zealand, UK	Fiji, Australia, New Zealand
Kiribati		
Export partners:	Australia, New Zealand, Japan	EC, Marshall Islands, US, American Samoa
Import partners:	Australia	Australia, Japan, New Zealand, UK, US
Vanuatu		
Export partners:	--	Netherlands, France, Japan, Belgium
Import partners:	--	Australia, Japan, New Zealand, France, FRG
Nauru		
Export partners:	Australia, New Zealand, Japan	Australia, New Zealand, Japan
Import partners:	Australia, Netherlands, New Zealand	Australia, UK, New Zealand, Japan

APPENDIX (continued)

Major Export and Import Partners of Pacific Rim Region Members For 1978 and 1988

	1978	1988
Southeast Quarter		
Chile		
Export partners:	FRG, US, Japan, Brazil	US, Japan, FRG, Italy
Import partners:	US, Brazil, Iran, Japan	US, Japan, FRG, France
Ecuador		
Export partners:	US, Japan, Chile	US, Panama, Coloymbia, Taiwan, EC
Import partners:	US, Japan, FRG, Italy	US, Japan, Brazil, FRG
Western Samoa		
Export partners:	--	France, US, Italy, New Caledonia, Japan
Import partners:	--	France, US, Other EC, Japan
Peru		
Export partners:	US, Japan, FRG, Yugoslavia	US, Japan, FRG, USSR, UK
Import partners:	US, FRG, Japan, Netherlands	US, FRG, Japan, Argentina, Brazil

APPENDIX (continued)

Major Export and Import Partners of Pacific Rim Region Members For 1978 and 1988

	1978	1988
Northeast Quarter		
United States		
Export partners:	Canada, Japan, Mexico, UK	Canada, Japan, Mexico, UK, FRG
Import partners	Canada, Japan, Saudi Arabia, Mexico	Japan, Canada, FRG, Taiwan, Mexico
Canada		
Export partners:	US, Japan, UK	US, European Community, Japan
Import partners	US, Japan, Saudi Arabia, UK	US, European Community, Japan
Mexico		
Export partners:	US, Spain, Japan	US, EC, Japan, Brazil
Import partners:	US, Japan, FRG	US, EC, Japan, FRG
Guatemala		
Export partners:	US, El Salvador, FRG, Nicaragua	US, El Salvador, Japan, FRG, Honduras
Import partners:	US, Venezuela, Japan, Netherland Antilles	US, FRG, Mexico, Venezuela
Honduras		
Export partners:	US, FRG, Canada, Guatemala	US, FRG, Japan, Guatemala, Panama
Import partners:	US, Japan, Venezuela, Guatemala	US, Japan, Mexico, Guatemala, FRG
El Salvador		
Export partners:	US, FRG, Guatemala, Netherlands	US, FRG, Guatemala, Japan
Import partners:	US, Guatemala, Venezuela, Japan	US, Guatemala, Mexico, Venezuela
Nicaragua		
Export partners:	US, FRG, China, Costa Rica	Japan, EC, US, CACM
Import partners:	US, Venezuela, Costa Rica, Guatemala	CACM, US, EC, E. Europe

APPENDIX (continued)

Major Export and Import Partners of Pacific Rim Region Members For 1978 and 1988

	1978	1988
Costa Rica		
Export partners:	US, FRG, Guatemala, El Salvador	US, UK, FRG, Japan
Import partners:	US, Japan, Guatemala, Venezuela	US, Japan, FRG, Venezuela
Panama		
Export partners:	US, Costa Rica, Netherlands, FRG	US, Costa Rica, FRG, Belgium
Import partners:	US, Saudi Arabia, Japan, Venezuela, FRG	US, Mexico, Japan, Ecuador
Colombia		
Export partners:	US, FRG, Venezuela, UK	US, FRG, Venezuela, Japan
Import partners:	US, Japan, Venezuela, FRG	US, Japan, FRG, Venezuela

Source: International Monetary Fund. *Direction of Trade Statistics*. Various Editions: 1989, 1988, and 1984. Washington, D.C.

INDEX

ABOUT THE AUTHOR

Chuck Dangler is the operations coordinator of his own diversified international market management company providing management options and international market information for businesses and private investors engaged in international business. He received his undergraduate education from The Evergreen State College in Olympia, Washington, and received his graduate education from Ohio University in international affairs.